Reason to Believe

The Philosophical and Personal Journeys of Atheists Who Discovered God

Sawsan Charif

Brain Corner Publishing

Copyrights

Copyright © 2025 by Sawsan Charif

All rights reserved.

No portion of this book may be reproduced in any form without written permission from the publisher or author, except as permitted by U.S. copyright law.

This publication is designed to provide accurate and authoritative information in regard to the subject matter covered. It is sold with the understanding that neither the author nor the publisher is engaged in rendering legal, investment, accounting or other professional services. While the publisher and author have used their best efforts in preparing this book, they make no representations or warranties with respect to the accuracy or completeness of the contents of this book and specifically disclaim any implied warranties of merchantability or fitness for a particular purpose. No warranty may be created or extended by sales representatives or written sales materials. The advice and strategies contained herein may not be suitable for your situation. You should consult with a professional when appropriate. Neither the publisher nor the author shall be liable for any loss of profit or any other commercial damages, including but not limited to special, incidental, consequential, personal, or other damages.

Book Cover by Sawsan Charif

Dedication

To my brilliant student and thought partner, Josep

A gifted scientist, a multilingual thinker, and a lifelong learner, your presence in my classroom quickly grew into something far more meaningful: a friendship grounded in curiosity, dialogue, and mutual respect. You brought a rare combination of analytical precision and philosophical depth to every conversation. As an English student with a formidable scientific mind and fluency in several languages, you challenged me to stretch beyond the boundaries of what I thought I knew—not only about science and spirituality, but about communication, belief, and the nature of understanding itself.

You helped me see that belief doesn't have to contradict reason; it can complement it, challenge it, and sometimes even complete it. Your questions sharpened my arguments. Your doubts strengthened my convictions. And your insights, whether offered with curiosity or caution, served as sparks that lit many pages of this book.

Our discussions—ranging from quantum theory to the existence of God—often left us with more questions than answers. Yet, in that shared space of inquiry, the spirit of this book was born. This project exists, in part, because you inspired me to write it.

Thank you—for your brilliance, your humility, your questions, and your unwavering pursuit of what is real.

Prologue

Heart Over Mind

A Reflection on the Threshold of Belief

There are moments in life—quiet, insistent moments—when something shifts inside us. A soft whisper beneath the noise. A sudden stillness in the chaos. These moments don't shout. They invite. And when they come, they don't ask for permission—they ask for presence.

For some, this moment is born of pain. For others, it arrives in beauty too vast to explain. For me, it came in silence—on a birthday that felt less like celebration and more like awakening. Not to answers, but to questions that echoed deeper than before.

I know what I'm about to say may be seen as controversial. But controversy no longer frightens me. Fear, after all, is a prison crafted by the mind—while freedom begins when we return to the heart.

We live in a world that worships intellect. We admire the sharp mind, the clever rebuttal, the evidence-based conclusion. And rightly so. But when reason becomes our only compass, we forget how to feel the wind.

There is a wisdom older than words. A knowing that predates dogma. Sages across traditions—Sufi mystics, Buddhist monks, Stoic philosophers, Indigenous elders—have all whispered the same truth: the deepest truths are not *thought*; they are *felt*. Not just believed, but *remembered*.

Faith, then, is not the abandonment of reason—but its evolution. It is what happens when the mind has reached its limits and the heart steps forward to guide the way.

I have come to believe that belief itself is not weakness. It is not surrendering to the irrational. It is surrendering to something *beyond* reason—something that reason, in its finest form, points toward.

This book is not a sermon. It is a searchlight. It is for the philosopher who finds themselves restless. For the skeptic who lies awake wondering if there's more. For the soul who no longer fits neatly into the boxes of disbelief, yet is afraid to step into the open air of wonder.

This is not a demand for agreement. It is an invitation.

As you turn these pages, may you feel safe enough to question, open enough to consider, and brave enough to follow the evidence wherever it leads—even if it leads somewhere unexpected.

Not all who believe were raised in belief. Some of us arrived here by accident, by crisis, or by awe. However you've come, you're welcome here.

And if you're standing on the edge of something—unsure, curious, quietly yearning—then you're exactly where you need to be.

Contents

Introduction

In 1966, Time magazine famously asked on its cover, "Is God Dead?" The question sent shockwaves through society, capturing a growing sentiment among many intellectuals that the concept of God was no longer relevant or defensible. Among those who embraced this view was Antony Flew, a renowned British philosopher and atheist who had long argued against the existence of a divine being. Yet, in a stunning reversal that made headlines around the world, Flew announced in 2004 that he had come to believe in God, citing the complexity of DNA and the origins of life as key factors in his transformation. It's worth noting that Flew embraced deism—belief in a creator based on reason and nature—rather than theism with its personal, intervening God, though his journey nonetheless illustrates how philosophical inquiry can lead to reconsidering the divine

Flew's journey from atheism to theism is not an isolated case. Throughout history, there have been numerous examples of individuals who, through a combination of reason, science, and personal experience, have found themselves drawn to belief in a higher power. From C.S. Lewis, the brilliant Oxford scholar who moved from skepticism to faith, to Francis Collins, the geneticist who led the Human Genome Project while also embracing Christianity, these stories challenge the assumption that faith and reason are inherently incompatible.

This book, "Reason to Believe," explores the intellectual and personal journeys of atheists who discovered God, providing insights into why and how these transformations occurred. It is important to note that the purpose of this work is not to "convert" anyone but rather to examine how some individuals have arrived at faith through a process of rational inquiry and lived experience. By delving into the philosophical arguments, scientific evidence, and personal testimonies that have led many to reconsider their atheistic worldviews, we aim to demonstrate that belief in God can be both intellectually sound and profoundly transformative.

Our target audience is adult atheists who find themselves questioning the presence of God, as well as those who consider themselves "spiritual but not religious." We recognize the intellectual curiosity and philosophical engagement that often characterize these individuals, and we seek to provide a thoughtful, balanced narrative that appeals to skeptics, seekers, and believers alike. This book is an invitation to explore both logic and lived experiences, not a demand for agreement but an encouragement for deep reflection.

Throughout the following chapters, we will examine the interplay between reason and faith, beginning with an exploration of the intellectual arguments that have led some atheists to reconsider their positions. From there, we will shift our focus to the personal experiences and epiphanies that have catalyzed spiritual awakenings, before finally examining the impact of belief on morality, meaning, and society as a whole. Each section builds upon the previous one, creating a compelling and cohesive narrative that challenges preconceptions and invites readers to consider new perspectives.

As an author, my passion for this subject stems from a deep desire to help others overcome skepticism and achieve a more profound understanding of faith. Having grappled with questions of belief and unbelief myself, I have come to appreciate the transformative power of a worldview that embraces both reason and transcendence. Through extensive research and engagement with a diverse range of sources, I aim to present a nuanced and intellectually rigorous exploration of these themes, one that respects the complexity of the human experience while also offering hope and insight.

Ultimately, "Reason to Believe" is an invitation to embark on a journey of discovery, one that challenges readers to approach the big questions of life with an open mind and a willingness to engage with ideas that may push them outside their comfort zones. As you read these pages, I encourage you to ponder your own beliefs and experiences, and to consider the possibility that faith and reason are not mutually exclusive but rather complementary facets of a rich and meaningful existence. In the end, perhaps the most important question is not whether God exists but rather what we are truly seeking in our quest for truth and purpose. Are we willing to follow the evidence wherever it leads, even if it means reconsidering our most deeply held convictions?

Chapter One

The Intellectual Landscape of Belief

Have you ever pondered how we humans, from the dawn of civilization, have been driven by an insatiable curiosity to understand our place in the universe? This journey, marked by an evolving tapestry of belief, reveals much about our collective psyche. Consider a time when early humans, surrounded by the mysteries of nature, sought explanations for the world around them. They saw spirits in the rustling leaves and divine forces in the roaring thunder. This primal worldview laid the foundation for the development of more complex theistic structures as human societies grew and evolved.

The Historical Evolution of Theism

As societies expanded and organized into more complex structures, so did their religious beliefs. The transition from animism to polytheism marked a significant shift in human thought. Polytheism, characterized by the worship of multiple gods, allowed for a more structured understanding of natural phenomena. Different deities became associated with various aspects of life—agriculture, war, love—and worship practices became more formalized.

The move from polytheism to monotheism represented another monumental shift in religious thought. Monotheistic beliefs, centered around the worship of a single, all-powerful deity, began to emerge in the Middle East. Judaism, Christianity, and Islam each presented a distinct vision of monotheism, emphasizing a personal relationship with a singular divine being. This transition allowed for a more unified theological narrative, which resonated deeply with the human desire for order and meaning in a chaotic world.

The Enlightenment era brought a wave of intellectual and cultural transformation that profoundly impacted religious thought. Enlightenment thinkers emphasized reason, scientific inquiry, and individual rights, challenging traditional religious authorities. This period saw the rise of deism, a belief in a non-interventionist creator, which reflected the era's focus on rationality and empirical evidence. The Enlightenment encouraged a critical examination of religious beliefs, leading to a growing emphasis on personal faith and spiritual autonomy.

Throughout history, these shifts in religious thought have been guided by key figures whose insights have shaped the development of theistic beliefs. Their contributions reflect the dynamic interplay between cultural context, intellectual inquiry, and spiritual experience that continues to influence our understanding of belief today.

Philosophical Groundwork: From Atheism to Theism

When you begin exploring the philosophical foundations of theistic belief, you'll encounter several compelling arguments that have guided thinkers through the centuries. The Cosmological Argument—one of the most intuitive—suggests that everything that begins to exist has a cause. When you follow this chain of causation backward, you eventually reach what philosophers call a "first cause" or "unmoved mover," which many identify as God. This argument appeals to your sense of logic; after all, in your everyday experience, events don't simply happen without causes.

Another cornerstone you'll discover is the Ontological Argument, which takes a different approach. Rather than looking at the physical world, it examines the very concept of God. The argument suggests that if we can conceive of a perfect being, such a being must exist, as existence would be a necessary attribute of perfection. While more abstract than other arguments, it invites you to consider whether the very idea of God implies more than just a hypothetical concept.

The Moral Argument connects the existence of objective moral values to a divine lawgiver. When you recognize certain actions as objectively right or wrong—not just matters of personal or cultural preference—this argument suggests you're perceiving a moral reality that requires explanation. C.S. Lewis, once an atheist himself, found this reasoning particularly compelling as he grappled with questions of right and wrong, ultimately concluding that moral law implies a moral lawgiver.

These philosophical approaches aren't just abstract theories—they've guided real people through profound shifts in belief. Consider the journey of Antony Flew, once a prominent atheist philosopher who later came to accept the existence of God. His transition wasn't based on religious experience but on philosophical and scientific reflection, particularly regarding the complexity of DNA and the origins of life. For Flew, the intricate information encoded in DNA suggested an intelligence behind the universe, illustrating how philosophical reasoning can lead to significant changes in worldview.

As you engage with these arguments, you're participating in a centuries-old conversation about the nature of existence and meaning. Whether you find them compelling or not, they offer intellectual pathways that have led many from skepticism to belief, demonstrating that faith need not be opposed to reason but can develop through thoughtful inquiry and reflection.

Rational Discourse vs. Dogma

In the vast landscape of human thought, you'll find the line between rational discourse and dogma can often blur. Yet distinguishing between the two is crucial for meaningful dialogue about belief. Rational discourse invites you to engage with open-minded exploration, a willingness to consider evidence, and respectful exchange of ideas. It thrives on questioning and diverse perspectives, allowing you to explore complex ideas without being constrained by predetermined conclusions. Dogma, in contrast, roots itself in rigidity, often refusing to consider alternative viewpoints or evidence that challenges established beliefs.

The hallmark of rational discourse lies in its foundation of logical consistency and evidence-based reasoning. When you engage in such discussions, you commit to critical thinking, evaluating arguments for their coherence and alignment with empirical evidence. This approach not only fosters a deeper understanding of differing viewpoints but also cultivates your own curiosity and humility. It encourages you to ask questions, seek clarity, and embrace the possibility of being wrong—traits that stand in stark contrast to dogmatic thinking.

Imagine joining a group discussing the existence of God at a local café. Among them is a scientist who values empirical evidence, a philosopher intrigued by metaphysical questions, and a theologian who draws from spiritual texts. Each brings a unique perspective to the table. Through respectful engagement, you could explore these ideas without pressure to conform to a single viewpoint. This exchange exemplifies rational discourse, where diverse perspectives enrich understanding and challenge assumptions.

You may have encountered misconceptions that faith and reason are mutually exclusive, yet history shows their harmonious coexistence. Philosophical arguments for God's existence, supported by historical evidence and reasoned inquiry, demonstrate that faith need not be blind or irrational. In fact, many thinkers have found their religious beliefs strengthened, rather than undermined, by rational exploration. These approaches to faith illustrate that belief can be both intellectually satisfying and spiritually fulfilling, bridging the perceived gap between reason and spirituality.

Intellectual Curiosity and the Quest for Understanding

Intellectual curiosity drives us to question our beliefs and seek deeper understanding. It often begins with simple but profound questions: What is the meaning of life? Why are we here? This pursuit of meaning transcends cultural and religious boundaries, touching on the essence of what it means to be human. For many, the search for coherence in understanding the universe becomes a lifelong endeavor, leading them to examine various belief systems, including theistic perspectives that offer answers to these age-old questions.

Your education and exposure to diverse knowledge play crucial roles in shaping your belief systems. Access to a wide range of academic disciplines encourages critical thinking and open-minded exploration. In university settings, you might encounter new ideas and worldviews that challenge your preconceived notions. For example, studying philosophy could introduce you to arguments for God's existence that you had never considered. Similarly, exposure to different cultures and religious practices can broaden your perspective, fostering an appreciation for the richness and diversity of human belief.

Consider the case of Francis Collins, a renowned geneticist who began as a staunch atheist. Through his study of the cosmos and the complexities of the universe, particularly DNA, he found himself drawn to questions that science alone couldn't answer. The intricate complexity of DNA, with its elaborate information system, suggested to him a design that prompted reconsideration of his stance on the existence of a higher power. His intellectual curiosity, paired with rigorous scientific inquiry, led him to explore the possibility of a divine creator—a journey shared by many scientists who have found that their pursuit of knowledge ultimately led them to a place of faith.

Bridging Science and Spirituality

The intersection of science and spirituality is often portrayed as a battlefield, yet history and contemporary thought reveal a more harmonious relationship. When you examine the compatibility of evolution with theistic belief, you'll find that many see no contradiction between the two. Evolution, the process by which life diversifies through natural selection, doesn't necessarily preclude the existence of a divine creator. Instead, for some believers, it illustrates the method by which a creator operates. This perspective allows for a nuanced understanding where scientific explanations of life's complexity and religious beliefs about creation coexist, each offering insights into the majesty of the universe.

Scientists who have embraced spiritual beliefs provide compelling examples of how these realms can enrich each other. Francis Collins, whom we mentioned earlier, exemplifies this synthesis. As head of the Human Genome Project, Collins found that his scientific work deepened rather than diminished his faith. He argues that the intricacies of DNA, the blueprint of life, reflect a grand design. For him, the pursuit of scientific truth illuminated his spiritual convictions, demonstrating that a life of faith need not reject empirical evidence.

Theological interpretations of scientific concepts further highlight this compatibility. Consider the anthropic principle, which suggests that the universe's conditions are finely tuned to allow for human existence. Some theologians argue that this fine-tuning points to intentionality, a purposeful design that aligns with theistic beliefs. By exploring theological perspectives on scientific phenomena, you can find deeper meaning and context, enriching both your scientific understanding and spiritual reflections.

Encouraging dialogue between scientific and religious communities fosters mutual respect and understanding. Conferences and forums dedicated to this dialogue serve as platforms where scientists, theologians, and philosophers can engage in meaningful conversations. These gatherings allow for the exchange of ideas, challenging preconceived notions and inviting participants to consider perspectives beyond their own fields. By promoting interdisciplinary discussions, we create a space where curiosity and wonder thrive, and where the pursuit of knowledge is celebrated as a shared endeavor.

Reflection Exercise

As you conclude this chapter, take a moment to reflect on your own intellectual journey. Consider the beliefs that have shaped your understanding of the world and how they have evolved over time. What questions continue to intrigue you? How has exposure to different perspectives influenced your thinking? Journal your thoughts or discuss them with someone who might offer a different viewpoint. Remember, the quest for understanding is not about arriving at final answers but about embracing the journey of exploration with an open mind and heart.

Chapter Two

Philosophical Arguments for God

Imagine standing at the edge of a vast desert, each grain of sand a testament to the universe's mysteries. As you ponder the origins of such an immense and intricate expanse, you might find yourself drawn to the philosophical question of causation—a question that has intrigued thinkers for centuries. This quest for understanding is at the heart of the cosmological argument, a cornerstone of theistic philosophy that seeks to explain the existence of the universe through the necessity of a first cause. The argument begins with the premise that everything that exists must have a cause. This chain of causation, if traced back, demands a starting point—a first mover or uncaused cause, often identified as God.

The principle of sufficient reason underpins this argument, asserting that everything must have an explanation, whether it be in the nature of a necessary being or an external cause. The distinction between contingency and necessity is crucial here. Contingent beings depend on something else for their existence, while a necessary being exists by its own nature, independent and self-sustaining. The cosmological argument posits that the universe, being contingent, requires a necessary being to account for its existence. This necessary being, transcending physical limitations, is what many conceptualize as God.

Historically, the cosmological argument has evolved through the contributions of prominent thinkers such as Thomas Aquinas and Gottfried Wilhelm Leibniz. Aquinas, in his "Five Ways," presented variations of this argument, each articulating different aspects of causation and necessity. He argued that the existence of motion, causation, and contingency in the world points to the necessity of a first cause or unmoved mover, which he equates with God. Leibniz, on the other hand, emphasized the principle of sufficient reason, arguing that the existence of the universe demands an explanation that cannot be found within the universe itself, thus pointing to an external, necessary being.

In modern times, the cosmological argument faces critiques from both scientific and philosophical perspectives. The challenge of infinite regress questions whether the universe requires a beginning or can exist eternally without a first cause. Quantum physics, with its exploration of particles that seem to emerge without clear causation, further complicates traditional notions of cause and effect. These critiques raise important questions about the nature of causality and the limitations of human understanding. The dialogue between science and philosophy offers a fertile ground for exploration, inviting us to reconsider our assumptions and expand our perspectives.

Despite these challenges, the cosmological argument remains a significant part of contemporary discourse on theism. It continues to provoke thought and discussion, encouraging both believers and skeptics to grapple with the profound questions of existence. Its enduring relevance lies in its ability to bridge the gap between empirical inquiry and philosophical reflection, offering insights into the nature of reality and our place within it. Whether viewed as a compelling testament to the existence of God or a starting point for further questioning, the cosmological argument invites us to engage with the mysteries of the universe in a meaningful and thoughtful way.

Reflection Section

Consider the principle of sufficient reason and how it might apply to your understanding of the universe. Reflect on whether you view the universe as contingent or necessary and how this perspective shapes your beliefs about existence. How do the concepts of causation and necessity resonate with your understanding of the world? Take a moment to jot down your thoughts and consider discussing them with someone who holds a different perspective.

The Role of Rationalism in Belief Systems

Rationalism is a philosophy where reason is the primary source of knowledge, and it plays a significant role in evaluating belief systems. At its core, rationalism advocates for the use of logical reasoning to analyze and understand the world. This approach can bridge the gap between atheism and theism by providing a common ground where belief and skepticism can engage in meaningful dialogue. Logical reasoning, with its emphasis on coherent arguments and evidence, allows individuals to weigh the merits of different perspectives, fostering a thoughtful exploration of faith. In discussions about religion, rationalism encourages you to ask questions, seek evidence, and critically assess the claims presented. It promotes an environment where ideas can be exchanged openly, challenging the notion that faith and reason are inherently incompatible. By emphasizing the importance of rational thought, you are invited to explore religious beliefs with an analytical mindset, considering both the logical and emotional dimensions of faith.

The relationship between rational thought and religious faith is often misunderstood as being mutually exclusive. However, throughout history, many have found ways to reconcile the two, demonstrating that faith can be grounded in reason. Rational arguments supporting theism often draw on philosophical principles, historical evidence, and experiential insights to make their case. For instance, the argument from design appeals to the intricate complexity of the universe as evidence of a purposeful creator. These arguments invite you to consider the possibility that faith is not merely wishful thinking but can be supported by logical reasoning. They challenge you to reflect on the assumptions underlying your beliefs, encouraging a deeper investigation into the nature of existence. By engaging with rational arguments, you may discover that faith can coexist with reason, each enriching the other and providing a more comprehensive understanding of the world.

Key figures in the history of philosophy have successfully integrated rationalism with their theistic beliefs, offering compelling examples of how reason and faith can coexist harmoniously. Blaise Pascal, a 17th-century mathematician and philosopher, famously argued for the rationality of belief in God through his "Wager." Pascal posited that, when faced with uncertainty, it is more rational to believe in God, as the potential benefits outweigh the risks of disbelief. His argument illustrates how reason can guide decisions about faith, even in the absence of empirical certainty. Alvin Plantinga, a contemporary philosopher, has also contributed to the philosophy of religion by exploring the rational foundations of theistic belief. Plantinga's work on "properly basic beliefs" suggests that belief in God can be rationally justified without requiring evidence, similar to how we accept the reliability of our senses. These thinkers demonstrate that rationalism and theism are not mutually exclusive but can inform and support one another in the pursuit of truth.

Despite these examples, rational objections to theism persist, often centered on the challenge of providing empirical evidence for religious beliefs. Critics argue that faith lacks the tangible proof required to validate its claims, leading to skepticism about its rationality. However, proponents of rational theism provide counterarguments that emphasize the limitations of empirical evidence in addressing metaphysical questions. They argue that, just as we accept certain truths without direct proof—such as the existence of other minds or the reality of the external world—faith can be a rational response to experiences and intuitions that transcend empirical verification. This perspective encourages you to consider the broader context of belief, recognizing that rationality encompasses not only evidence but also philosophical reflection and personal insight. By engaging with these counterarguments, you may find that the rationality of faith lies in its ability to address the profound questions of existence, offering a framework for understanding the mysteries of life.

The Ontological Argument: Logic and Faith

Imagine pondering the very nature of existence and arriving at the conclusion that the mere concept of God implies His reality. This is the essence of the ontological argument, a philosophical assertion introduced by Anselm of Canterbury. Anselm proposed that God, being the greatest conceivable being, must exist not only in the mind but also in reality. The logic follows that a God who exists solely as an idea would be less than a God who exists in actuality, as existing in reality is greater than existing merely as a concept. This argument doesn't rely on physical evidence but instead on the power of reason, challenging you to rethink what it means to believe in God.

Critics have long debated the logical validity of the ontological argument, highlighting both its strengths and weaknesses. Gaunilo of Marmoutier famously critiqued Anselm's reasoning with his "perfect island" analogy. He argued that if Anselm's logic held, one could conceive of the most perfect island, and by that logic, it must exist. This illustration aimed to show the flaw in defining things into existence through mere conceptualization. Meanwhile, Immanuel Kant offered a different critique, arguing that existence is not a predicate or quality that can be attributed to a being. For Kant, saying something exists doesn't add to its nature or enhance its attributes. These critiques force a reevaluation of the argument's structure, inviting deeper reflection on what it means to claim that God must exist.

Despite these challenges, the ontological argument has been reformulated over the centuries to address its criticisms. Alvin Plantinga introduced a version using modal logic, which considers the possibility of worlds other than our own. Plantinga's version suggests that if it is possible for a maximally great being to exist, then such a being exists in some possible world. If this being exists in any possible world, it must exist in all possible worlds, including ours. This approach attempts to bypass some of the traditional critiques by introducing new layers of logical complexity, offering a fresh perspective on an age-old argument.

The ontological argument's significance lies not just in its logical structure but in its ability to bridge faith and reason. By engaging with this argument, you are prompted to consider the nature of existence and the role of conceptual thought in understanding the divine. It challenges you to explore the boundaries of logic and belief, questioning how ideas and reality intersect. The argument has influenced theological and philosophical thought, sparking discussions on the nature of God and the limits of human understanding. While it may not compel you to believe, it invites you to engage with foundational questions about what it means to exist and how we comprehend the divine.

The Teleological Argument: Design in Nature

Picture a finely crafted watch, its gears and springs intricately aligned to keep precise time. This analogy, known as the watchmaker analogy, has long been used to illustrate the teleological argument, which posits that the complexity and order observed in the universe suggest the presence of an intelligent designer. Just as a watch implies a watchmaker, the argument suggests that the universe's intricate mechanisms point toward a purposeful creator. The regularity of planetary orbits, the precision of physical constants, and the complexity of biological systems all contribute to this sense of deliberate design. The universe, in its vastness and detail, seems too finely tuned to be the product of random chance, prompting the question: could such complexity arise without a guiding hand?

Historically, the teleological argument has evolved through various interpretations. In the 18th century, William Paley famously articulated the watchmaker analogy in his work, "Natural Theology," arguing that the natural world, with its intricate systems and harmonious order, pointed to the existence of a divine designer. Paley's argument resonated with many who saw evidence of intentional design in nature's complexity. In modern times, the fine-tuning argument has emerged, building on Paley's ideas by focusing on the precise conditions necessary for life. Modern cosmology reveals that the universe's fundamental constants appear calibrated to allow for the existence of life, suggesting a level of design that some argue points to an intelligent creator.

Critiques of the teleological argument often hinge on the role of natural selection and evolutionary processes in explaining complexity. Darwin's theory of evolution provides a powerful counterargument, proposing that the diversity and complexity of life can be attributed to natural processes rather than a designer. Evolutionary biology suggests that complex structures and behaviors can emerge through gradual adaptations over time, driven by environmental pressures. However, proponents of the teleological argument counter with the concept of irreducible complexity, which posits that certain biological systems are too complex to have evolved incrementally. They argue that some systems require all parts to function, suggesting the necessity of an intelligent designer to account for their existence. This debate continues to spark intense discussions about the mechanisms underlying complexity and the role of a designer in nature.

The influence of the teleological argument extends into both scientific and religious communities, shaping debates on topics like intelligent design. In education, discussions about intelligent design often center on its place within science curricula, with proponents arguing for its inclusion alongside evolutionary theory. Critics, meanwhile, contend that intelligent design lacks empirical support and should not be taught as science. These debates highlight broader tensions between scientific explanations and religious interpretations, prompting questions about the nature of evidence and the boundaries of scientific inquiry. In religious circles, the teleological argument continues to inspire reflection on the relationship between faith and the natural world, inviting believers to consider how the perceived design in nature might reflect divine intent. Such reflections encourage ongoing exploration of the intersections between science and spirituality, as individuals seek to understand the universe and their place within it.

Moral Arguments: Ethics Without God?

When contemplating the essence of morality, one encounters a profound question: Do objective moral values and duties suggest the presence of a moral lawgiver? This inquiry forms the basis of the moral argument for God's existence. The argument posits that objective moral values—principles that hold true regardless of personal beliefs or cultural perspectives—imply a source beyond human convention. In contrast, subjective morality is shaped by individual or societal preferences, lacking universal applicability. Proponents of the moral argument assert that objective moral laws, which bind us to concepts of right and wrong, hint at a divine origin. Without a transcendent source, they argue, moral values become relative, shifting with social trends and personal whims.

Throughout history, philosophers have championed the moral argument, each contributing unique insights. Immanuel Kant, renowned for his exploration of moral philosophy, introduced the idea of the "moral law within." Kant believed that a sense of duty and morality was innate, guiding individuals beyond self-interest. He argued that this internal moral compass pointed to a higher source, suggesting that moral obligations are not merely human constructs. C.S. Lewis, a 20th-century thinker and former atheist, also made significant contributions with his argument from morality. Lewis observed that a universal sense of right and wrong, shared across cultures, indicated a moral standard beyond human invention. For him, this standard pointed to the reality of a divine lawgiver, grounding morality in something greater than human consensus.

Yet, the moral argument faces challenges from secular perspectives that offer alternative explanations for ethics. Evolutionary biology, for instance, suggests that moral instincts evolved to promote cooperation and survival. Traits like empathy and altruism could have developed as advantageous behaviors, fostering group cohesion and increasing chances of survival. In this view, moral tendencies are natural outcomes of evolutionary processes, not divine mandates. Additionally, moral relativism posits that moral values are shaped by cultural influences and social norms, varying across societies and historical contexts. This perspective challenges the notion of objective morality, proposing that ethics are fluid and context-dependent, rather than fixed and universal.

The implications of these debates reach far into contemporary ethical discussions and societal values. Religion plays a significant role in moral education, often shaping the ethical frameworks within which individuals and communities operate. For many, religious teachings provide foundational moral principles, guiding behavior and decision-making. This influence extends into broader societal norms, where religious values intersect with secular laws and policies, contributing to the ongoing dialogue about the nature of ethics and morality. The interaction between religious and secular perspectives enriches the discourse, encouraging critical examination of the sources and justifications for moral claims. Through this exploration, we are invited to consider the complexities of moral reasoning, questioning how our understanding of ethics aligns with our beliefs about the divine.

The Existential Argument: Meaning and Purpose

Consider the search for meaning, a fundamental human quest that drives much of our thought and action. The existential argument posits that belief in God provides a framework for meaning and purpose in life, addressing our deepest questions about existence. Without such a framework, life can seem arbitrary, a series of random events devoid of significance. For many, the absence of a divine reference point leaves a void, a sense of being adrift in an indifferent universe. Belief in God, however, offers a narrative that situates individual lives within a larger, purposeful context. It suggests that existence is not merely accidental but part of a grand design, imbuing life with direction and significance.

The existentialist movement, with its focus on individual experience and meaning, offers varied perspectives on this quest. Søren Kierkegaard, a pivotal figure in existentialist thought, introduced the concept of the "leap of faith." For Kierkegaard, faith was not a conclusion reached through logical deduction but a personal commitment, a choice to believe despite uncertainty. This leap of faith acknowledges the limits of reason, embracing the possibility of a transcendent purpose. In contrast, Jean-Paul Sartre, an atheistic existentialist, rejected the notion of an inherent meaning bestowed by God. Sartre argued that existence precedes essence, meaning humans are free to create their own purpose. This freedom, while liberating, also brings the weight of responsibility, as individuals must construct meaning in a world without predefined values. These existential perspectives highlight the diversity of thought on meaning and purpose, illustrating how belief in God or its absence shapes one's understanding of existence.

The human desire for purpose is a driving force behind many of our actions and aspirations. A sense of purpose provides direction, guiding decisions and instilling a sense of fulfillment. Research has shown that perceived purpose positively impacts mental health, contributing to greater life satisfaction and resilience. Those who find meaning in their lives often report higher levels of well-being and are better equipped to cope with adversity. The existential argument suggests that belief in God offers a robust foundation for such purpose, aligning individual goals with a greater cosmic plan. This alignment can foster a sense of belonging and continuity, connecting personal experiences to a larger narrative that transcends individual existence.

In modern discourse, the existential argument continues to resonate, influencing both philosophical and spiritual movements. In an era marked by rapid change and uncertainty, the quest for meaning remains a central concern. Contemporary thinkers explore how belief systems, both theistic and secular, address this existential need. Spiritual movements often draw on the existential argument to offer frameworks for understanding life's purpose, encouraging individuals to explore their beliefs and values in pursuit of meaning. These discussions reflect the ongoing relevance of existential questions, inviting you to consider how your beliefs shape your understanding of purpose and direction.

As we conclude this chapter on philosophical arguments for God, it's clear that questions of meaning and purpose are central to human experience. The existential argument, along with the other arguments explored, invites reflection on the nature of belief and its role in shaping our lives. These philosophical inquiries set the stage for the next chapter, where we will delve into the psychological aspects of belief, examining how faith intersects with identity, emotion, and cognition.

Chapter Three

Cosmology and Fine-Tuning

The Big Bang and Divine Creation

In the annals of scientific discovery, few theories have reshaped our understanding of the universe as profoundly as the Big Bang Theory. This scientific explanation posits that the universe began as an infinitely dense point, or singularity, and has been expanding ever since. This singularity, a concept at the heart of cosmology, represents a time when the laws of physics as we know them break down. The evidence for this theory is compelling, particularly the cosmic microwave background radiation—an all-pervading afterglow of the initial explosion, which serves as a relic of the universe's fiery birth. This radiation, uniformly spread throughout the cosmos, provides a snapshot of the infant universe, supporting the notion that all matter and energy were once compacted in a singular, explosive event. The Big Bang Theory not only explains the observable expansion of the universe but also frames our understanding of its origins within a narrative that is both scientific and evocative.

This theory's implications for religious creation narratives are as vast as the cosmos itself. For many religious traditions, including Christianity, the idea of a universe with a definitive beginning resonates with creation stories. For instance, the Genesis account in the Bible describes a divine act that brings forth the heavens and the earth from a state of void. Some theologians and believers find harmony between the Big Bang Theory and Genesis, viewing the scientific account as complementary to the metaphorical language of scripture. They argue that both narratives describe a universe brought into existence from nothing, a concept known as creatio ex nihilo. However, not all religious interpretations align with this view. Some see the Big Bang as conflicting with literal interpretations of sacred texts, leading to debates within religious communities about how to reconcile scientific findings with traditional beliefs.

The dialogue surrounding the Big Bang Theory extends beyond religious texts, engaging diverse perspectives from both scientific and religious communities. Theistic evolutionists, for example, embrace the Big Bang as part of a divine plan, seeing God as the initiator of the cosmic event and the subsequent unfolding of natural laws. They argue that the universe's orderly expansion and the emergence of life reflect intentionality and purpose. In contrast, some atheists view the Big Bang as evidence of a naturalistic universe, governed by chance and the laws of physics without the need for supernatural intervention. For these individuals, the universe's emergence from a singularity underscores the power of scientific inquiry to unravel the mysteries of existence without recourse to divine explanations.

The debate over the universe's fine-tuning adds another layer to this discourse. The fine-tuning argument posits that the universe's fundamental constants and physical laws are precisely calibrated to allow for the existence of life. Proponents argue that this precise calibration suggests divine intervention, as the likelihood of such conditions arising by chance is astronomically low. This perspective is bolstered by the anthropic principle, which states that the universe's laws appear fine-tuned for the emergence of observers like us. The anthropic principle has theological implications, suggesting that the universe is configured in a way that supports life, potentially pointing to a purposeful creator. Yet, this view is not without its critics. Some scientists propose multiverse theories, suggesting that our universe is just one of many, each with different physical laws. In this context, fine-tuning might be an inevitable outcome in a vast ensemble of universes, where only those capable of supporting life are observed.

Chapter Four

Biology, Consciousness, and Complexity

Imagine standing beneath the vast night sky, peppered with stars that have fascinated humanity for millennia. For centuries, these celestial bodies have inspired wonder and inquiry, guiding explorers, poets, and scientists in their quest to understand the universe. Astronomy, with its profound ability to reveal the depths of the cosmos, often serves as a bridge between the empirical and the spiritual. One cannot gaze upon the infinite expanse without pondering life's grander questions. It is in these moments of awe that science and belief intersect, offering a stage for the dance of intellect and faith. This chapter explores how scientific discoveries have shaped and challenged religious beliefs, inviting you to consider the dual role of science as both skeptic and affirming muse.

The discovery of DNA, the very blueprint of life, has captivated both scientists and theologians alike. The intricate complexity of DNA, with its precise sequences and elegant structure, has led some to argue for intelligent design—a notion that the complexity of life is indicative of a purposeful creator. Proponents of intelligent design suggest that such complexity could not arise from random processes alone, pointing to the possibility of a guiding hand. Whether or not you embrace this view, the debate around DNA's origins underscores the broader dialogue between science and belief. It challenges preconceived notions and invites deeper inquiry into the origins of life, encouraging a nuanced perspective that values both scientific rigor and philosophical reflection.

The Hubble Telescope offers another lens through which to view the universe's majesty. By capturing images of galaxies billions of light-years away, it has expanded our understanding of cosmic vastness and complexity. These discoveries prompt reflection on humanity's place in the universe, inspiring both wonder and humility. For some, the vastness revealed by the Hubble Telescope affirms the possibility of a creator, suggesting that such grandeur might be the work of a divine architect. For others, it reinforces a sense of existential curiosity, fueling the quest for knowledge and understanding. By providing a glimpse into the universe's scale, the Hubble Telescope invites a dialogue between science and spirituality, offering endless opportunities for exploration.

Science's dual role as both questioner and affirming force is evident in its ability to challenge and reinforce religious beliefs. Scientific skepticism often prompts reassessment of faith, encouraging believers to critically evaluate their convictions. This process can lead to a more mature and nuanced understanding of belief, one that embraces both doubt and certainty. Simultaneously, scientific discoveries can evoke a sense of awe and wonder, inspiring spiritual reflection and deepening one's appreciation for the mysteries of existence. This interplay between skepticism and awe highlights the dynamic relationship between science and faith, inviting you to explore the intersections where they converge and diverge.

Religious communities have responded to scientific discoveries in various ways, often adapting their beliefs to accommodate new insights. The Catholic Church's acceptance of evolutionary theory illustrates this adaptability, as it reconciles scientific understanding with theological doctrine. By embracing evolution, the Church acknowledges the compatibility of scientific inquiry with religious belief, fostering a dialogue that respects both domains. This willingness to integrate scientific discoveries into religious frameworks demonstrates the potential for harmony between science and spirituality, encouraging open-minded exploration and mutual respect.

Consider the story of an astronomer whose faith was profoundly influenced by scientific knowledge. Initially skeptical of religious claims, their study of the cosmos led to a profound sense of wonder and questioning. The beauty and order they observed in the universe prompted them to reconsider their stance on the existence of a higher power. This transformation illustrates the capacity of scientific inquiry to inspire spiritual reflection, challenging assumptions and inviting a reevaluation of deeply held beliefs. Through the lens of astronomy, they found a new perspective on faith, one that harmonizes scientific understanding with spiritual insight.

Reflection Section

Think about a moment when a scientific discovery or experience inspired you to question or reassess your beliefs. How did this influence your perspective on faith and reason? Reflect on how the interplay between science and spirituality can enrich your understanding of the world and your place within it. Consider jotting down your thoughts or discussing them with a friend for further exploration.

The Neuroscience of Spiritual Experiences

Within the human brain lies a complex network that not only governs our daily functions but also plays a key role in our spiritual experiences. Neuroscience offers a fascinating lens through which to explore spirituality, providing insights into how our brains perceive and process these profound experiences. Neuroimaging studies of meditation and prayer have revealed that certain brain regions, such as the prefrontal cortex and the temporal lobe, become highly active during spiritual practices. The prefrontal cortex, associated with focus and decision-making, shows increased activity, suggesting a state of heightened awareness and concentration. Meanwhile, the temporal lobe, linked to sensory perception and emotional response, often lights up during these spiritual activities. This activation can lead to feelings of connection and transcendence, experiences that many describe as deeply spiritual. For some, these findings offer a biological explanation for spiritual experiences, suggesting that our brains are wired to seek and interpret the divine.

The relationship between spirituality and mental health is another area where neuroscience provides valuable insight. Spiritual practices such as mindfulness and meditation have been shown to have positive effects on mental health, reducing symptoms of anxiety and depression. Mindfulness, which involves maintaining a present-focused awareness, helps individuals manage stress by promoting relaxation and emotional regulation. Studies have shown that regular mindfulness practice can lower cortisol levels, a hormone associated with stress, and increase the production of serotonin, a neurotransmitter linked to mood regulation. Similarly, the placebo effect—where belief in a treatment's efficacy can lead to real improvements—has been observed in religious contexts, where faith and expectation can enhance well-being. These findings suggest that spirituality, whether through belief or practice, can have tangible benefits for mental health, offering individuals a means of coping with life's challenges.

However, the materialist perspective offers a different interpretation of these phenomena. Materialists argue that spiritual experiences are purely neurological events, the result of chemical reactions and electrical impulses within the brain. From this viewpoint, what we perceive as spiritual is merely the brain's way of interpreting complex sensory and emotional data. Reductionist interpretations often strip spirituality of its mystery, reducing it to neural activity without deeper significance. Critics of this perspective, however, argue that it fails to account for the richness and depth of spiritual experiences. They contend that while neuroscience can describe the processes underlying these experiences, it cannot fully capture their meaning and impact on human life. This debate highlights the tension between scientific explanation and spiritual interpretation, inviting further exploration of the boundaries between the two.

Neuroscience's exploration of spirituality has implications for personal belief systems and the broader dialogue between science and religion. As scientific understanding of the brain's role in spirituality grows, it challenges traditional notions of faith, prompting believers to reconsider the nature of their spiritual experiences. For some, science enhances their faith, offering a framework to understand the divine's workings in the material world. Others might find their beliefs challenged, leading to a reevaluation of their spiritual convictions. This ongoing dialogue between neuroscience and theology enriches both fields, offering new perspectives on age-old questions about the nature of belief and the divine. By examining the biological underpinnings of spirituality, we gain a deeper appreciation for the complex interplay between our physical and spiritual selves, inviting reflection on the profound mysteries of consciousness and existence.

Quantum Physics and the Question of God

In the realm of the very small, quantum mechanics governs reality in ways that challenge our everyday understanding. It suggests that quantum systems exist in a superposition of states until they are measured, at which point they assume a definite state—a phenomenon known as the observer effect. This effect arises from the interaction between a quantum system and a measuring apparatus, not necessarily from conscious observation, though interpretations of its implications remain a subject of ongoing debate. Nevertheless, the idea that observation can affect outcomes has led some to explore deeper philosophical and theological questions about the role of consciousness in shaping reality. Quantum entanglement, another cornerstone of quantum theory, reveals a profound interconnectedness between particles, such that a change in one instantaneously affects the other, regardless of distance. This phenomenon challenges our traditional notions of space, time, and causality, offering fertile ground for spiritual interpretations that emphasize unity, connection, and the mysterious oneness underlying all things.

As quantum theory unfolded in the early 20th century, various interpretations emerged, each with unique implications. The Copenhagen interpretation, favored by Niels Bohr and Werner Heisenberg, posits that a quantum system remains in a state of superposition until observed, at which point it collapses into a definite state. This perspective has spurred philosophical musings about the role of the observer, leading some to draw parallels with the concept of a divine observer or consciousness. On the other hand, the Many-Worlds interpretation, proposed by Hugh Everett, suggests that all possible outcomes of quantum measurements are realized in branching parallel universes. While dazzling in its implications, this interpretation challenges traditional notions of a singular, ordered creation, inviting philosophical debate on the nature of existence and reality.

However, the allure of quantum mechanics also brings the risk of quantum mysticism, where scientific concepts are misappropriated to justify spiritual claims without rigor or clarity. Critics of quantum mysticism argue that the misuse of quantum terminology can lead to confusion and pseudoscience, undermining both scientific integrity and theological discourse. It is crucial to distinguish between legitimate scientific inquiry and speculative interpretations that lack empirical support. By maintaining scientific rigor, one can appreciate the genuine mysteries of quantum mechanics without resorting to unfounded claims that blur the line between science and spirituality.

Some theologians have embraced the challenge of integrating quantum concepts into their understanding of God, developing what is sometimes called quantum theology. They explore the idea of God as the ultimate observer, whose consciousness brings the universe into being, much like an observer collapsing a quantum state. This perspective suggests that God's omnipresence and omniscience are consistent with the interconnectedness and non-locality observed in quantum mechanics. While these interpretations remain speculative, they offer a fresh lens through which to consider the divine, inviting dialogue between scientific discovery and theological reflection.

In navigating the complex terrain of quantum mechanics and its implications, one must tread carefully, balancing curiosity with skepticism. Quantum mechanics continues to challenge our understanding of reality, offering insights that provoke both wonder and debate. As we explore these ideas, we are reminded of the vastness of the unknown and the potential for discovery that lies at the intersection of science and theology.

Evolution, Morality, and the Divine

Evolution is one of the most profound scientific theories, fundamentally altering our understanding of life on Earth. It proposes that all species of organisms arise and develop through natural selection, which favors traits that enhance survival and reproduction. This process, combined with common descent—the idea that all living beings share a common ancestor—paints a picture of life as a dynamic, interconnected tapestry. Such a view has challenged traditional religious beliefs that envision creation as a singular, divine act. For some, the notion that life evolved without direct divine intervention seems to contradict religious narratives. Yet, the power of evolution lies not only in its ability to explain the diversity of life but also in its capacity to provoke new interpretations of faith and existence.

The implications of evolutionary theory extend beyond biology, influencing our understanding of morality and ethics. Evolutionary biology suggests that traits like altruism and cooperation have evolved because they enhance the survival of species. Altruism, the selfless concern for others, can be seen as benefiting group cohesion and success. Similarly, moral instincts—innate senses of right and wrong—might have evolved to foster social harmony and cooperation. These ideas challenge the belief that morality is solely a divine gift, suggesting instead that ethical behavior could be a product of evolutionary pressures. However, this does not diminish the moral frameworks that religions provide. Instead, it invites a dialogue between secular and religious perspectives on the origins of morality, encouraging a richer understanding of human ethics.

The view known as theistic evolution offers a bridge between science and religion, positing that evolution is a tool used by a divine being to bring about life. This perspective allows for the reconciliation of evolutionary science with the belief in a purposeful creator. Francis Collins, a prominent advocate of theistic evolution, argues that God's creation of life through evolution does not diminish the divine but rather displays the elegance and complexity of God's methods. Collins, a geneticist and devout Christian, sees no contradiction between his scientific work and his faith. For him, the discovery of evolution enhances his appreciation for the divine intricacy of creation. Such perspectives illustrate that belief in God and acceptance of evolutionary science can coexist harmoniously, offering a worldview that respects both the evidence of science and the insights of faith.

The debate over divine influence in evolution remains a lively and contentious one. Some advocate for intelligent design, which suggests that certain features of the universe and living things are best explained by an intelligent cause rather than an undirected process like natural selection. Proponents argue that the complexity and functionality observed in nature indicate a designer's hand. In contrast, others support the idea of unguided evolution, asserting that natural processes alone are sufficient to explain life's diversity without invoking divine intervention. This debate raises fundamental questions about the role of a creator in the natural world and whether evolution inherently excludes or includes divine influence. For those who question the presence of God, this conversation invites exploration into how science and faith can inform and enrich one another, challenging assumptions and expanding the boundaries of understanding.

As we conclude this chapter on the science of belief, it's clear that the intersections of evolutionary theory, morality, and divine influence provoke deep reflection on the nature of existence. Each perspective offers valuable insights, encouraging a dialogue that respects the complexities of both science and faith. With these thoughts in mind, we transition to the next chapter, where we will explore personal testimonies and the powerful stories of those who have navigated the path from atheism to belief.

Chapter Five

The Psychological Aspects of Belief

Imagine standing at the crossroads of a bustling city, where each street represents a different path of thought, belief, and understanding. At every turn, the cacophony of voices, ideas, and convictions surrounds you, each vying for attention, each presenting a narrative that claims to make sense of the world. This is the realm of belief, where psychology plays an intricate role in guiding the choices and pathways we take. There, cognitive dissonance acts as a silent architect, shaping belief systems by helping individuals justify their sacrifices and commitments, even when faced with contradictory evidence. This phenomenon, as explored by Wendy Ulrich in her work on religious experience, reveals how the discomfort of holding opposing views drives people to resolve tensions by altering their beliefs or perceptions. It underscores the human tendency to seek consistency, which can lead to embracing beliefs that align with one's actions, even if those beliefs require a leap of faith.

Another powerful cognitive mechanism is confirmation bias, the tendency to favor information that supports existing beliefs while dismissing evidence to the contrary. This mental shortcut streamlines decision-making but can also entrench individuals in their convictions, making it challenging to objectively evaluate competing viewpoints. For those questioning the presence of God, awareness of confirmation bias invites a more critical approach to examining spiritual claims, urging a willingness to engage with diverse perspectives and evidence. Such introspection can be both liberating and unsettling, as it necessitates confronting long-held assumptions and embracing the complexity of human thought. Understanding these cognitive processes highlights the importance of cultivating an open mind, one that remains receptive to new ideas while acknowledging the biases that shape our perceptions.

Beyond cognitive mechanisms, motivational factors play a crucial role in belief formation. At the heart of many belief systems lies the human need for certainty, especially during uncertain times. Beliefs offer a framework of understanding, providing a sense of security and predictability amidst the chaos of life. This desire for existential security often drives individuals to adopt beliefs that promise stability and coherence, offering solace in the face of life's unpredictability. Moreover, the longing for community and belonging further influences belief systems, as shared beliefs foster social cohesion and identity. This sense of belonging can be particularly appealing to those who feel isolated or disconnected, serving as a powerful motivator for embracing particular ideologies or spiritual practices.

Psychological theories offer valuable insights into why people gravitate toward specific belief systems. Maslow's hierarchy of needs, for instance, suggests that once basic physiological and safety needs are met, individuals seek fulfillment through love, esteem, and self-actualization. Maslow later introduced the concept of transcendence, recognizing spirituality as a means of achieving a higher purpose beyond the self. This theory underscores the role of spirituality in satisfying deeper psychological needs, aligning with the quest for meaning and connection that often accompanies belief. Similarly, attachment theory sheds light on the emotional underpinnings of religious affiliations, positing that early relationships influence one's perception of the divine. Individuals with secure attachments may view God as a loving, supportive figure, while those with insecure attachments might experience religious guilt or anxiety, reflecting their interpersonal dynamics.

Research on the relationship between belief and mental health reveals both positive and negative effects. Studies indicate that religious practices can reduce stress, offering psychological benefits through rituals that promote relaxation and emotional regulation. Engaging in prayer or meditation, for instance, can lower cortisol levels, alleviate anxiety, and enhance well-being. These practices provide a structured means of coping with life's challenges, reinforcing resilience and mental fortitude. However, the psychological impact of belief is not universally positive. Religious guilt and anxiety can arise from rigid doctrines or judgmental communities, exacerbating stress and hindering personal growth. This duality highlights the nuanced relationship between belief and mental health, emphasizing the need for balanced perspectives that consider both the supportive and constraining aspects of religious engagement. For those exploring their beliefs, acknowledging this complexity invites a deeper understanding of how belief systems influence psychological well-being, offering opportunities for reflection and growth.

Reflection Exercise

Consider a belief or conviction you hold strongly. Reflect on the cognitive processes, such as confirmation bias or cognitive dissonance, that may influence your perspective. Do you seek out information that supports your beliefs while dismissing opposing evidence? How do your beliefs fulfill deeper psychological needs, such as community or certainty? Take a moment to journal your thoughts, exploring how these insights may impact your understanding of belief and its role in your life.

Existential Anxiety and the Search for Meaning

In the quiet moments of reflection, when the noise of daily life subsides, you might find yourself grappling with a profound sense of existential anxiety. This is a feeling that arises from the awareness of life's inherent uncertainty and the vast, indifferent universe that surrounds us. It's the unease that comes from questioning your place in a world where meaning isn't readily apparent. Without a predefined framework to guide you, the pursuit of purpose becomes a daunting task. The challenge lies in constructing a personal narrative that infuses life with significance, a process that requires introspection and courage. This quest for meaning can feel overwhelming, as traditional sources of stability and direction may no longer suffice, leaving you to confront the vastness of existence with little more than your own convictions and insights.

Finding ways to cope with existential anxiety is crucial for personal growth and resilience. One effective strategy is to engage in mindfulness practices that anchor you in the present moment. Techniques such as meditation and deep breathing can help quiet the mind, allowing you to focus on the here and now rather than becoming lost in the uncertainty of the future. These practices cultivate a sense of peace and acceptance, offering a respite from the relentless quest for certainty. Additionally, creative activities provide an expressive outlet, enabling you to explore emotions and ideas in ways that words alone cannot capture. Whether it's painting, writing, or playing music, creativity allows you to channel your inner turmoil into something tangible and meaningful. These activities foster a sense of agency and empowerment, reminding you that while the universe may be vast and indifferent, your capacity to create and express is boundless.

Consider the story of a woman named Claire, who found herself at a crossroads following a major life transition. With her children grown and her career winding down, she faced an existential crisis that left her questioning her identity and purpose. In search of answers, Claire turned to writing as a form of expression, pouring her thoughts and reflections into a journal. Through this process, she discovered a new passion for storytelling, which not only provided her with a sense of purpose but also connected her with others who shared similar experiences. Claire's story illustrates the transformative power of creative exploration in navigating existential anxiety and finding meaning in unexpected places.

Belief systems can also play a significant role in alleviating existential anxiety by providing structure and meaning. Religious rituals, for example, offer a sense of comfort and stability through their familiar patterns and symbols. They create a framework that helps individuals navigate life's uncertainties, offering reassurance in the face of the unknown. These rituals often serve as reminders of a larger narrative, one that situates personal struggles within a broader context of faith and community. For those who find solace in spiritual practices, belief systems offer a refuge from the chaos of existence, grounding them in a sense of purpose and belonging. This connection to a greater whole can be a powerful antidote to the isolation and uncertainty that often accompany existential anxiety.

Spiritual Experiences Without a Deity

Imagine standing at the edge of a vast canyon, where the earth opens up to reveal its ancient story, carved by time and elements. In this moment, you feel a profound sense of awe, a connection to something greater than yourself, yet without the confines of religious doctrine. This is the essence of non-theistic spirituality, where experiences of wonder and transcendence occur independently of belief in a deity. It's a form of spirituality that thrives in the natural world, where the beauty and complexity of nature evoke feelings of reverence and interconnectedness. These experiences, though not tethered to a god, are rich with meaning, offering a sense of peace and belonging in a chaotic world.

Meditation and mindfulness are practices that embody non-theistic spirituality, focusing on the present moment and fostering a deep awareness of self and surroundings. Through meditation, you cultivate a calm and centered state, reducing stress and anxiety, and enhancing emotional regulation. These practices are not about escaping reality but engaging with it more fully, allowing you to experience life with clarity and intention. The benefits of meditation extend beyond mental health; they touch on the spiritual, providing a framework for exploring one's inner landscape without the need for religious belief. In this way, spirituality becomes a personal journey of growth and self-discovery, tailored to individual needs and experiences.

Across cultures, spirituality without a deity takes on diverse forms, each reflecting unique traditions and values. Indigenous spiritual practices, for instance, often center around nature, viewing the earth as sacred and alive with spiritual significance. These traditions emphasize harmony with the natural world, encouraging practices that honor the interconnectedness of all living things. Secular humanism offers another perspective, focusing on human potential and ethical living without reliance on supernatural beliefs. This approach to spirituality emphasizes the importance of reason and compassion, fostering a sense of purpose and meaning grounded in human experience. Both examples illustrate how spirituality can be a rich and varied tapestry, woven from the threads of cultural heritage and personal insight.

Research into non-theistic spirituality reveals its growing prevalence and impact, particularly among those who identify as spiritual but not religious (SBNR). Surveys indicate that individuals in this category often report high levels of life satisfaction and well-being, attributing their sense of fulfillment to spiritual practices that resonate with their values and beliefs. The SBNR movement reflects a shift towards individualized spirituality, where personal experiences and insights guide one's spiritual path. This trend highlights the adaptability and inclusivity of spirituality, accommodating a wide range of beliefs and practices that transcend traditional religious boundaries.

Reflection Exercise

Consider a moment when you felt a deep sense of awe or connection to something greater. Reflect on how this experience shaped your understanding of spirituality and its role in your life. Write down your thoughts and explore how non-theistic spirituality might offer a path to personal growth and fulfillment, independent of religious doctrine.

Reconciliation of Belief and Identity

Imagine your identity as a mosaic, each piece representing varied beliefs, experiences, and values. As you navigate life's twists, these pieces shift, sometimes harmonizing beautifully, other times clashing. Belief systems play a pivotal role in shaping this mosaic, influencing how you see yourself and how others perceive you. Religion, for many, is a cornerstone of cultural belonging, providing a sense of identity and community. Yet, when beliefs evolve, the once-cohesive mosaic can fracture, creating internal conflict and a struggle for coherence. This tension is familiar to those who question the presence of God, as they grapple with reconciling past convictions with new insights. Such identity conflicts are often compounded by external pressures, where societal expectations or familial traditions clash with personal growth. In these moments, the challenge lies in finding a balance, allowing your identity to adapt and change without losing its essence.

Reconciling conflicting beliefs with your sense of identity is a nuanced process, requiring intentional reflection and openness. One effective strategy is integrating diverse belief elements into a cohesive identity, much like blending colors on an artist's palette to create a new hue. This approach involves embracing contradictions as opportunities for growth, allowing seemingly disparate beliefs to coexist and inform one another. It encourages you to draw from various traditions and philosophies, crafting an identity that is both unique and unified. Support from interfaith or secular communities can also play a crucial role in this reconciliation process. These communities offer safe spaces for exploration and dialogue, where diverse perspectives are valued and respected. Engaging with others who share similar struggles provides empathy and understanding, reinforcing the notion that identity is fluid and ever-evolving.

Consider the story of Alex, who grew up in a devout religious household but found themselves questioning core tenets of their faith. Initially, this questioning led to feelings of isolation and confusion, as Alex feared losing their sense of belonging. However, through participation in an interfaith discussion group, Alex discovered that others shared similar experiences and doubts. This community provided a platform for Alex to explore diverse beliefs, ultimately embracing a pluralistic identity that honored both their heritage and newfound perspectives. Alex's journey highlights the transformative power of community support in reconciling identity conflicts, illustrating how shared experiences foster resilience and belonging.

A stable sense of identity significantly influences the stability of belief systems. When you possess a robust identity, it acts as a protective anchor during times of doubt and uncertainty. This stability allows you to approach new ideas without fear of losing yourself, fostering an environment where exploration is encouraged and welcomed. In contrast, an unstable identity can render you vulnerable to external pressures, swaying your beliefs with every passing breeze. Therefore, cultivating a strong sense of self is crucial for maintaining belief stability, providing a foundation upon which diverse ideas can build. This doesn't imply rigidity but rather a dynamic strength that accommodates change while remaining grounded in core values.

In essence, identity and belief are intertwined, each shaping and informing the other. As you navigate the complexities of belief and identity, remember that this process is not about finding definitive answers but embracing the journey of discovery and growth. Your identity is a living tapestry, constantly evolving as you engage with the world and its myriad possibilities. Each thread, whether old or new, contributes to the richness of your experience, weaving a narrative that is uniquely yours.

Overcoming Fear of Judgment

Navigating the world with beliefs that diverge from the mainstream can be daunting. Society often champions conformity, and stepping outside its boundaries can invite scrutiny. This scrutiny frequently originates from family expectations, where tradition and cultural norms hold significant sway. Families may impose implicit or explicit pressures to align with long-standing beliefs, which can create tension for those seeking to explore alternative perspectives. Cultural conformity extends beyond familial circles, permeating social interactions and community dynamics, where deviation from the norm is met with skepticism or outright disapproval. This environment fosters a fear of judgment, where the potential for social rejection looms large, impacting one's willingness to express unique beliefs.

This pervasive fear can have profound psychological effects, contributing to anxiety and stress. The mere anticipation of negative judgment can lead to avoidance behaviors, where individuals might suppress their true beliefs to maintain social harmony. This suppression, however, exacts a toll on mental well-being, as living inauthentically breeds internal conflict and dissatisfaction. Anxiety stemming from perceived social rejection can manifest in various ways, including heightened stress levels, decreased self-esteem, and a diminished sense of belonging. Over time, these psychological impacts can erode one's confidence and stifle the pursuit of genuine self-expression, creating a cycle of fear and withdrawal.

To overcome the fear of judgment, cultivating strategies that bolster self-confidence in one's beliefs is crucial. Cognitive-behavioral techniques offer valuable tools for challenging negative thought patterns that fuel fear and insecurity. By identifying and reframing irrational beliefs, individuals can develop a more balanced perspective, reducing the emotional grip of fear. Additionally, building supportive networks of like-minded individuals can provide a sanctuary where diverse beliefs are celebrated rather than scrutinized. These communities offer validation and encouragement, reinforcing the notion that differing perspectives enrich rather than detract from the human experience. Engaging with others who share similar values fosters a sense of belonging and empowerment, countering the isolating effects of judgment.

Consider the stories of individuals who have faced judgment yet emerged with resilience and confidence. Public figures who advocate for minority belief systems often exemplify this strength, using their platforms to challenge prevailing norms and inspire others. Figures like Malala Yousafzai or Greta Thunberg have faced significant criticism for their activism, yet their unwavering commitment to their beliefs has galvanized global movements. These narratives of resilience highlight the power of conviction and the importance of standing firm in one's beliefs, even in the face of opposition. They remind us that embracing authenticity, while challenging, ultimately paves the way for meaningful change and personal fulfillment.

Ending with these reflections, we see how overcoming the fear of judgment is not a solitary endeavor but a collective movement toward acceptance and understanding. As we conclude our exploration into the psychological aspects of belief, consider how these insights might inform your journey. Embracing the complexities of belief and identity opens the door to growth and transformation, setting the stage for our next chapter, where the interplay between faith, reason, and ethical living takes center stage.

Chapter Six

Personal Testimonies: Journeys from Atheism to Belief

In the intricate tapestry of human experience, few threads are as compelling as the personal stories of those who shift from atheism to belief in God. These narratives are often marked by moments of profound realization—turning points that challenge the certainties held by the mind and stir the depths of the soul. Such moments can emerge from the most unexpected places, as illustrated by the life of C.S. Lewis. Once a staunch atheist shaped by personal loss and philosophical skepticism, Lewis experienced a transformative epiphany, not through dramatic revelation, but through a series of quiet reflections and intellectual encounters. This journey culminated in a reluctant admission of belief, as he described himself as being "the most dejected and reluctant convert in all England." His story resonates with many who have found themselves grappling with the tension between doubt and faith, reason and intuition.

The turning point in a person's journey toward belief often begins with a crisis that shakes the foundations of atheistic certainty. Consider the case of an individual facing a life-altering health scare. Faced with their own mortality, they found themselves drawn to spiritual reflection, seeking comfort and meaning beyond the material world. This crisis opened the door to new possibilities, prompting them to explore spiritual texts and engage with religious figures who offered solace and guidance. This encounter with spirituality was not an immediate conversion but rather the beginning of a journey marked by questioning and curiosity. Through internal debates and philosophical questioning, they began to entertain the idea that perhaps there was more to existence than they had previously acknowledged.

Personal experiences, more than abstract concepts, often drive the shift from atheism to theism. Witnessing acts of kindness and selflessness can serve as a powerful catalyst, challenging the notion that life is merely a series of random events. For one individual, observing the unwavering compassion of a religious community during a time of need sparked an internal dialogue about the nature of goodness and the source of moral values. These experiences, coupled with personal moments of perceived divine intervention, led to a reevaluation of their beliefs. In these instances, the heart often speaks louder than the mind, compelling individuals to explore the spiritual dimensions of life.

Community support plays a vital role in nurturing the budding belief. The influence of a mentor—someone who provides guidance and encouragement—can be transformative. Through regular conversations with a spiritual guide, one might find clarity and direction, as the mentor shares insights and perspectives that illuminate the path to faith. Participation in faith-based group activities further reinforces this journey, offering a sense of belonging and shared purpose. Being part of a community that values compassion, humility, and service can create an environment where belief flourishes, supported by the collective strength of like-minded individuals.

Reflection Section

Consider a moment in your life when a personal experience challenged your beliefs. How did this experience shape your understanding of faith and reason? Reflect on the role of community in your life and how it has influenced your journey. You may find it helpful to journal your thoughts or discuss them with someone you trust.

These stories of conversion are as diverse as the individuals who live them, yet they share common elements of doubt, reflection, and personal transformation. They remind us that belief is not a linear trajectory but a dynamic process influenced by a myriad of factors. As we delve into these personal testimonies, we are invited to consider the transformative power of belief and the unique paths that lead individuals to embrace faith.

Stories of Intellectual Transformation

In the realm of intellectual discovery, the path from atheism to theism can be as intricate as the concepts themselves. For many, the transformation begins with a shift from a purely scientific worldview, where empirical evidence reigns supreme, to one that embraces the spiritual dimensions of existence. Consider the case of an academic deeply entrenched in the sciences, whose life was governed by the laws of physics and biology. Yet, as they delved into the complexities of the universe, the intricate patterns and unexplained phenomena prompted a reconsideration of their rigid stance. It wasn't a rejection of science, but an expansion of understanding that allowed room for the mysteries that science alone could not explain. This intellectual curiosity led them to explore philosophical texts that challenged the boundaries of atheism, engaging with ideas that suggested the presence of a higher order.

Educational settings often serve as fertile ground for such transformations. In the halls of universities, students encounter religious philosophy that prompts them to question previously held beliefs. A philosophy course might introduce them to the works of thinkers like Thomas Aquinas or Søren Kierkegaard, challenging them to consider the arguments for God's existence with fresh eyes. The exposure to diverse perspectives in academic discourse encourages them to grapple with concepts that transcend empirical evidence, inviting them into a dialogue that is as personal as it is intellectual. The university, with its vibrant exchange of ideas, becomes a place where belief systems are not only tested but also expanded, leading some to embrace a more theistic worldview.

Key influences and inspirations often play pivotal roles in these intellectual transformations. C.S. Lewis, once a resolute atheist, found his path to belief profoundly shaped by the works of authors like G.K. Chesterton, whose writings bridged the gap between skepticism and faith with eloquence and wit. These authors offered new lenses through which to view reality, suggesting that faith and reason are not adversaries but allies in the quest for truth. The writings of such thinkers provide a framework for understanding complex theological concepts, making them accessible to those who might otherwise dismiss them. Through these literary encounters, individuals find their resistance to theism gently eroded by the power of well-reasoned argument and imaginative insight.

Engagement in dialogues and debates further spurs this exploration. Participating in interfaith discussions provides a platform for exchanging ideas in an environment that values both challenge and respect. Here, individuals confront their assumptions head-on, prompted to articulate their beliefs with clarity and precision. These discussions, whether formal debates or casual conversations, offer insights that provoke deeper reflection and encourage the pursuit of knowledge beyond one's comfort zone. In this dynamic exchange, the seeds of transformation are planted, nurtured by the realization that belief is not a static state but a living, evolving understanding of the world and our place within it.

For those who question the presence of God, these stories of intellectual transformation offer a compelling narrative of reasoned inquiry leading to faith. They illustrate that the path to belief is not one of abandoning reason, but of expanding its reach to include both the seen and the unseen, the known and the mysterious.

In this journey of exploration, individuals are invited to embrace the complexities of existence, finding meaning and purpose in a worldview that welcomes both curiosity and wonder.

From Skepticism to Faith: A Testimonial

Among the varied narratives of finding faith, personal testimonies stand out for their raw, unfiltered accounts of transformation. Take the story of an individual who, after years of staunch atheism, found themselves drawn into a world of belief. Raised in an environment where skepticism was valued and religious sentiments were often dismissed, they had embraced a worldview rooted in rationality and evidence. However, a chance encounter with a well-reasoned argument for theism sparked a curiosity that could not be easily ignored. This individual began a cautious exploration, not expecting to find anything that would challenge their firmly held beliefs. Yet, as they engaged with philosophical ideas and theological discussions, their skepticism began to waver. They found that logical reasoning and evidence could coexist with faith, each enriching the other in unexpected ways.

The path from skepticism to belief is rarely smooth. It often involves overcoming numerous obstacles, both external and internal. For this individual, skepticism from peers was a significant challenge. Friends who had known them as a committed atheist found it difficult to accept their newfound interest in religion. This skepticism, rooted in shared history and mutual understanding, posed a formidable barrier. It required resilience to keep exploring beliefs that seemed to diverge from the collective identity of their social circle. Additionally, personal biases against religion, formed over years of critical thought, proved hard to shake. The journey required a willingness to confront these biases head-on, to question assumptions that had been held as self-evident truths. This process was not easy, but it was necessary for growth and understanding.

A pivotal aspect of this transformation was the role of evidence and reason. Encountering compelling arguments for theism—arguments that appealed to the intellect and resonated with the heart—played a significant part in reshaping their perspective. They found themselves captivated by the intricacies of philosophical arguments that suggested the existence of a higher power. The moral argument, which posits that objective moral values point to a moral lawgiver, struck a chord. It challenged them to consider the foundations of their ethical convictions and whether those values could exist independently of a divine source. Engaging with these ideas in depth, they discovered that reason and faith were not mutually exclusive but could inform and support one another in profound ways.

Throughout this transition, the emotional journey was equally significant. Moments of doubt were frequent, as old certainties clashed with emerging beliefs. There were times when the weight of skepticism felt overwhelming, threatening to derail the progress made. Yet, alongside these doubts were moments of resolution, where clarity emerged from the fog of uncertainty. These moments were characterized by a profound sense of peace and understanding, a feeling that the pieces of a complex puzzle were finally starting to align. This emotional roller-coaster, marked by highs and lows, was an integral part of the transformation. It added depth and authenticity to the experience, reinforcing the realization that belief is as much about the heart as it is about the mind.

In sharing this testimonial, the aim is not to present a one-size-fits-all narrative of conversion but to highlight the unique and personal nature of the journey from skepticism to faith. Each story is different, shaped by individual experiences, challenges, and revelations. Yet, common threads run through these narratives—threads of curiosity, resilience, and the search for meaning. They remind us that belief is a dynamic process, one that evolves as we engage with the world around us and the ideas within us.

The Emotional Path to Spiritual Awakening

The shift from atheism to belief is often fueled by powerful emotions that challenge the boundaries of logic and reason. Experiences of profound love or loss can act as catalysts, stirring a deep sense of vulnerability and introspection. Imagine the intense emotional weight that accompanies the loss of a loved one. In those moments, the finality of life confronts us with questions that logic struggles to answer. The heart seeks solace, and the mind yearns for a framework to understand the pain. For many, the embrace of faith offers a balm, providing a narrative that speaks to the continuity of existence and the promise of reunion. Through rituals and prayers, individuals find a means to express their grief, transforming it into a source of strength and resilience.

Moments of gratitude and awe also play a crucial role in awakening spiritual awareness. Standing before a breathtaking landscape, the sheer beauty of nature can invoke feelings of connection to something greater than oneself. This sense of wonder transcends the boundaries of the material world, inviting contemplation of the divine. In such moments, gratitude becomes a bridge to faith, encouraging a deeper appreciation for life's mysteries. The experience of awe, whether inspired by nature, art, or human kindness, opens the heart to possibilities beyond the empirical, nurturing a sense of spiritual curiosity and openness.

Faith often provides emotional healing during times of turmoil, offering strength and a renewed sense of purpose. Consider the solace found in prayer during periods of overwhelming grief. Prayer becomes a refuge, a space where emotions are acknowledged and held within the comforting embrace of belief. It offers a means of processing complex feelings, fostering a sense of peace that transcends the immediate circumstances. Additionally, the support of a faith community can be invaluable, offering companionship and understanding. Within this collective, individuals find empathy and solidarity, reinforcing the notion that they are not alone in their struggles. This communal support fosters resilience, empowering individuals to face life's challenges with courage and hope.

The emotional journey to faith often heralds personal growth and a shift in values. As belief takes root, priorities may realign, reflecting a new understanding of what truly matters. Material pursuits may give way to a focus on relationships, compassion, and service. This change is not merely a rejection of the old but an embrace of a richer, more meaningful perspective. Through faith, individuals find clarity and direction, guided by principles that resonate with their deepest convictions. This transformation reflects an evolution of the self, as new insights and experiences shape identity and purpose.

The joy of discovering faith is a deeply fulfilling experience, imbued with hope and optimism. Individuals often describe a sense of liberation, as if a veil has been lifted, revealing the world in vibrant colors. There is a newfound appreciation for life's beauty and potential, a recognition of the interconnectedness of all things. This joy is not the absence of challenges but the presence of a sustaining belief that infuses life with meaning. It is the quiet confidence that arises from knowing that, despite uncertainties, there is a guiding force that offers love and wisdom. This narrative of joy and fulfillment serves as an inspiring testament to the transformative power of faith, inviting others to explore the possibilities of a life enriched by belief.

Finding Community in Faith

The transition to belief is often enriched by the discovery of a supportive community. For those questioning the presence of God, joining a local church or faith group can offer a nurturing environment where questions are welcomed rather than judged. Imagine walking into a room filled with warm, welcoming faces, each person eager to share in your spiritual exploration. This sense of belonging is not just about attending services; it's about building friendships with fellow believers who share your values and aspirations. These relationships provide the encouragement needed to explore faith more deeply, creating a network of support that can be both comforting and inspiring. Through shared experiences, you find yourself growing alongside others, united by a common purpose and a desire to understand the divine.

Within this community, shared values and beliefs serve as a foundation that strengthens personal convictions. Participating in communal rituals and traditions, whether it be a weekly gathering or seasonal celebration, reinforces a sense of unity and continuity. These practices, steeped in history and meaning, offer a tangible connection to something greater than oneself. As you engage in these rituals, you may find your own beliefs becoming clearer, shaped by the collective wisdom of the community. This shared journey offers a sense of stability and direction, guiding you as you navigate the complexities of faith. The communal aspect of belief adds depth to your understanding, providing a framework within which you can explore your spirituality with confidence and clarity.

The impact of belonging to a faith community extends beyond the spiritual, influencing personal and emotional development as well. Feeling accepted and understood in a religious setting fosters a sense of security and self-worth. It allows you to express your beliefs without fear of judgment, encouraging authenticity and vulnerability. This acceptance can be transformative, helping you to embrace your identity as a believer while also respecting the diverse perspectives of others. The sense of belonging nurtures a supportive atmosphere where growth is encouraged, enabling you to explore your faith without constraint. This environment, rich in empathy and understanding, provides the foundation for a fulfilling and meaningful spiritual life.

However, integrating into a new faith community is not without challenges. Navigating cultural differences within the group requires sensitivity and resilience. You may encounter traditions or practices that are unfamiliar or even uncomfortable, demanding an open mind and willingness to adapt. This process of integration is a learning experience, one that fosters personal growth and broadens your understanding of the diversity within faith. Overcoming initial feelings of alienation or uncertainty is part of this journey, as you find your place within the community and discover how your unique perspective contributes to the collective whole. These challenges, though daunting, are opportunities for growth, inviting you to engage with the complexities of belief in a way that enriches your spiritual journey.

As this chapter draws to a close, it's clear that community plays a pivotal role in the transition to faith. The supportive network of a faith group provides the encouragement, stability, and shared wisdom necessary for personal and spiritual growth. Through these connections, you are invited to explore your beliefs with openness and curiosity, finding strength in the shared experiences and collective insight of those around you. This exploration of community sets the stage for the next chapter, where we will delve into philosophical arguments and the interplay of reason and belief, examining how intellectual exploration can further enrich the journey of faith.

Chapter Seven
Addressing Atheist Objections

Imagine a courtroom where evidence is presented and scrutinized, each piece weighed for its significance and reliability. In the realm of belief, the role of empirical evidence is akin to this process, serving as a pivotal factor in shaping our convictions about the existence of God. Yet, unlike the definitive verdicts of a courtroom, the conclusions we draw from empirical evidence in matters of faith are often more nuanced and complex. Empirical evidence encompasses a variety of forms, including historical records, scientific discoveries, and personal experiences, each offering unique insights into the divine's existence.

Historical evidence provides a rich tapestry of human encounters with the divine, as seen in the archaeological discoveries that corroborate historical religious texts. For instance, the discovery of the Dead Sea Scrolls offered tangible support for the historical accuracy of biblical narratives, reinforcing the authenticity of ancient religious accounts. These findings bridge the gap between sacred texts and historical reality, inviting us to consider the possibility of divine intervention in human history. Similarly, scientific evidence also plays a role in this dialogue. The study of cosmology, with its exploration of the universe's origins, often intersects with theological concepts, offering a framework for understanding creation that resonates with religious narratives. Yet, while these forms of empirical evidence provide valuable insights, they also reveal the limitations of relying solely on empirical verification.

The challenges of empirical evidence become apparent when we consider the limitations of scientific methodology in addressing metaphysical questions. Science, by its nature, is equipped to explore the physical world, offering explanations grounded in observation and experimentation. However, when it comes to questions of ultimate meaning, purpose, or the existence of a transcendent reality, science encounters its boundaries. These questions often reside in the domain of philosophy and personal belief, where empirical evidence alone may not suffice. The limitations of scientific inquiry in these areas highlight the need for a more holistic approach to understanding belief, one that integrates empirical findings with subjective experience and philosophical reasoning.

A balanced approach that respects both the insights of empirical evidence and the richness of personal experience can offer a more comprehensive understanding of belief. Personal experiences, such as moments of awe in nature or profound realizations during meditation, often play a crucial role in shaping our beliefs about the divine. These experiences, while subjective, carry a compelling authenticity that resonates with those who encounter them. They invite us to explore the spiritual dimensions of life, providing a complementary perspective to the empirical evidence that informs our understanding. Integrating philosophical arguments with empirical findings further enriches this exploration, allowing us to engage with complex ideas that transcend the limitations of any single discipline.

Empirical inquiry has, at times, aligned with religious beliefs in ways that foster a harmonious relationship between science and faith. Consider the numerous scientific studies that have explored the psychological and physical benefits of religious practices, such as prayer and meditation. These studies often reveal a correlation between spiritual practices and improved well-being, suggesting that faith can have tangible, positive effects on our lives. This alignment between empirical findings and religious beliefs underscores the potential for faith to enhance our understanding of the world, offering a framework that respects both the rigor of science and the depth of spirituality.

Reflection Section

Reflect on a time when empirical evidence, whether historical, scientific, or experiential, influenced your beliefs about the divine. How did this evidence shape your understanding of faith? Consider journaling about this experience, noting any questions or insights that arose as a result. This reflection can provide a foundation for further exploration, encouraging you to integrate personal experiences with empirical findings in your ongoing quest for understanding.

Beyond the God Delusion: Respectful Debate

In today's world, where discussions about belief often turn into fiery debates, the tone of popular atheist literature frequently influences the nature of these exchanges. Take Richard Dawkins's *The God Delusion*, a book that has sparked much discussion and controversy. Dawkins, with his incisive critique of religion, takes a confrontational stance, describing belief in God as a "delusion". While his arguments aim to challenge traditional views, the book's assertive tone often shuts down dialogue before it begins. This approach leaves little room for productive conversation, creating an environment where defensiveness flourishes instead of understanding. Critics have pointed out that while Dawkins's work is compelling in its logic, its aggressive rhetoric can alienate those who might otherwise be open to discussion.

This confrontational style is not exclusive to Dawkins. Many prominent atheist writers adopt a similar approach, which can lead to polarization rather than enlightenment. Such rhetoric tends to reinforce existing biases, making it difficult for individuals on either side of the belief spectrum to engage in meaningful dialogue. When the discourse becomes a battleground, the opportunity for mutual understanding diminishes. In these instances, the focus shifts from seeking truth to winning arguments, leaving little space for empathy or growth. The impact of such polarization is evident in the broader cultural landscape, where discussions about faith and belief often become divisive, rather than unifying.

To foster a more constructive dialogue, we must prioritize respect and understanding in our discussions. This means approaching conversations with empathy, recognizing that everyone's beliefs are shaped by personal experiences and perspectives. Active listening becomes crucial here—truly hearing what the other person is saying, rather than merely waiting for a chance to respond. It's about creating a space where ideas can be exchanged freely and thoughtfully, without fear of judgment or ridicule. Guidelines for civil discourse emphasize the importance of acknowledging the validity of differing viewpoints and engaging with them respectfully. This approach not only enriches the conversation but also builds bridges between individuals who might otherwise remain divided.

As we navigate these discussions, it's essential to be aware of how media and social platforms can amplify polarization. The echo chambers of social media often reinforce our biases, feeding us content that aligns with our existing beliefs while filtering out opposing views. This can create an illusion of consensus and further entrench divisions, making it challenging to consider alternative perspectives. In this environment, it's easy to lose sight of common ground, focusing instead on points of contention. To counteract this, we must actively seek out diverse viewpoints, challenging ourselves to engage with ideas that might initially seem foreign or uncomfortable.

One effective strategy for finding common ground is to focus on shared values and goals. Whether discussing ethics, morality, or the nature of existence, there are often underlying principles that both atheists and theists can agree upon. By emphasizing these commonalities, we create a foundation for dialogue that transcends ideological differences. Building on this shared foundation, we can explore the complexities of belief with openness and curiosity, rather than hostility. It's about recognizing that, despite our differences, we are all seeking answers to life's profound questions, and that these answers may be more nuanced and interconnected than they initially appear.

Constructive dialogue requires a willingness to engage with others in a spirit of collaboration rather than competition. Instead of viewing discussions as debates to be won, we should approach them as opportunities to learn and grow together. Techniques for fostering this collaborative mindset include asking open-ended questions, seeking clarification, and expressing genuine interest in understanding the other person's perspective. By doing so, we create an environment where everyone feels valued and heard, paving the way for meaningful exchanges that can lead to greater understanding and insight. Through such respectful dialogue, we can bridge the gaps that separate us, discovering new ways to connect and communicate amidst our diverse beliefs.

Exploring Agnosticism: A Middle Path

Imagine standing at a crossroads where certainty seems elusive and questions linger without easy answers. This is the realm of agnosticism, a middle path between theism and atheism that embraces uncertainty as a fundamental aspect of belief. Agnosticism, at its core, acknowledges the limits of human knowledge when it comes to the existence of a deity or the divine. Unlike atheism, which often asserts the non-existence of gods, or theism, which affirms their presence, agnosticism occupies a space where doubt and openness coexist. It is not simply indecision but a recognition that some questions may remain unanswered, at least for now.

Agnosticism manifests in different forms, often categorized as strong or weak. Strong agnosticism maintains that knowledge of God's existence is inherently unknowable, asserting that human understanding is too limited to address such profound mysteries. In contrast, weak agnosticism suggests that while we may not currently have the evidence to definitively prove or disprove the existence of God, it is not beyond the realm of possibility that such evidence could emerge. Both forms share a commitment to open inquiry, valuing the pursuit of knowledge over rigid conclusions. This approach allows agnostics to navigate the complex landscape of belief with curiosity and humility, remaining open to new insights and discoveries.

Philosophically, agnosticism is deeply rooted in skepticism and empiricism, traditions that emphasize questioning and evidence-based reasoning. Skepticism, with its insistence on critical examination, encourages agnostics to question assumptions and seek clarity in their understanding of the divine. Empiricism, which prioritizes sensory experience and observation, underscores the agnostic's reliance on tangible evidence while acknowledging the limitations of this approach in addressing metaphysical questions. Historical figures such as T.H. Huxley, who coined the term "agnosticism," have championed this perspective, advocating for a stance that respects the boundaries of human knowledge. Huxley's principle of agnosticism emphasizes the importance of withholding judgment in the absence of conclusive evidence, encouraging an openness to future possibilities.

The appeal of agnosticism lies in its embrace of uncertainty and its encouragement of intellectual humility. By acknowledging the limits of our understanding, agnostics cultivate a mindset that values inquiry and exploration. This openness fosters a willingness to engage with diverse perspectives, recognizing that truth may be multifaceted and complex. Agnosticism encourages a dialogue that respects differing beliefs, creating a space for constructive conversation rather than confrontation. In this way, agnostics contribute to a culture of curiosity and learning, where questions are celebrated as opportunities for growth rather than obstacles to be overcome.

However, the agnostic path is not without its challenges. One of the primary difficulties faced by agnostics is the tension between seeking certainty and accepting ambiguity. The human desire for answers can clash with the agnostic's commitment to uncertainty, creating a sense of restlessness or dissatisfaction. This tension requires a delicate balance, where the pursuit of knowledge is tempered by an acceptance of the unknown. Agnostics must navigate the complexities of belief and skepticism, often feeling caught between the definitive claims of theism and atheism. This position can sometimes lead to isolation, as agnostics are neither fully embraced by religious communities nor by staunch atheists.

Despite these challenges, the agnostic perspective offers valuable insights into the nature of belief and understanding. It reminds us that the pursuit of truth is an ongoing process, one that requires patience and perseverance. By embracing uncertainty, agnostics invite us to consider the possibilities that lie beyond our current understanding, encouraging a mindset that is both open and reflective. This approach fosters a culture of inquiry, where the search for meaning is not constrained by rigid boundaries but is instead guided by curiosity and wonder. In this way, agnosticism offers a path that respects the complexities of belief, inviting us to explore the mysteries of existence with an open heart and an inquisitive mind.

A Response to Atheist Critics

When addressing criticisms from atheists, it's crucial to understand the context behind their concerns. One of the most common criticisms lies in the perceived failures of religious institutions and practices. Many atheists point to historical events such as the Crusades or the Inquisition as examples of religion's potential to cause harm. These events highlight how religious institutions, when intertwined with political power, can sometimes stray from their spiritual ideals. Furthermore, some critics argue that religious dogma can impede scientific progress and individual freedoms, pointing to instances where religious beliefs have clashed with scientific advancements or human rights.

Another major point of contention is the concept of divine intervention. Critics often question the idea of a benevolent deity who intervenes in the world, especially in the face of widespread suffering and injustice. This skepticism is closely tied to the "problem of evil," which challenges the existence of an all-powerful, all-loving God in a world rife with pain. Atheists argue that if such a deity existed, they would prevent suffering or at least mitigate its impact. This line of reasoning leads many to conclude that the notion of divine intervention is either flawed or irrelevant.

In response to these criticisms, it is important to offer thoughtful counterarguments that rely on logic and evidence. Addressing the problem of evil, philosophers have proposed various theodicies. One such argument suggests that free will is central to the human experience, and that the potential for evil is a necessary consequence of granting humans the freedom to choose. Without free will, moral growth and genuine love would be impossible. Another perspective posits that suffering can lead to greater goods, such as compassion and resilience, which are integral to personal and spiritual development.

Beyond the philosophical realm, the historical and social contributions of religion cannot be overlooked. Religious institutions have played significant roles in shaping societies, providing education, healthcare, and social support throughout history. Many of the world's first universities and hospitals were founded by religious organizations, reflecting their commitment to social welfare. Moreover, religious teachings have inspired countless acts of kindness and altruism, motivating individuals to serve their communities and advocate for justice. It's crucial to acknowledge these positive contributions when evaluating the role of religion in society.

While atheists and theists may differ in their views on divinity, there are areas where both can find common ground. Ethical values, such as compassion, justice, and empathy, are often shared across belief systems. These values can serve as a foundation for collaboration on social justice initiatives and humanitarian efforts. By focusing on these shared goals, atheists and theists can work together to address pressing issues such as poverty, inequality, and environmental degradation. This cooperative spirit fosters a sense of unity and purpose, transcending ideological differences.

Encouraging ongoing dialogue and understanding between atheists and theists is vital in bridging divides and fostering mutual respect. Empathy and openness are key to this process, allowing individuals to appreciate the diversity of thought and experience that defines our world. Engaging in conversations with an open mind creates opportunities for learning and growth, challenging assumptions and broadening perspectives. By valuing each other's insights and experiences, we can cultivate an environment where differences are respected, and common values are celebrated.

Ultimately, embracing dialogue and cooperation enriches our understanding of belief and strengthens our collective capacity to create positive change. While the paths we walk may differ, the shared journey toward understanding and compassion can unite us in meaningful ways. In the chapters that follow, we'll explore the interplay of faith and reason, examining how these concepts can coexist and complement one another in our search for truth and meaning.

Chapter Eight

The Interplay of Faith and Reason

Imagine a tapestry, woven with threads of both faith and reason, each strand distinct yet inseparable, creating a coherent and complex whole. This image reflects the historical dance between these two forces, often seen as opposing but, in reality, deeply intertwined. In the medieval period, Thomas Aquinas, a towering figure in Christian theology, articulated a synthesis that set the stage for future discourse. Aquinas, drawing from Aristotle, argued that faith and reason were complementary paths to truth, each with its unique role in understanding the divine and the natural world. His "Summa Theologiae" remains a testament to this harmony, demonstrating that theological inquiry could coexist with and even be enriched by philosophical rigor. Aquinas believed that reason could lead us to certain truths about God, while faith completed the picture, revealing mysteries beyond human comprehension.

As we moved into the Enlightenment, thinkers like Immanuel Kant and John Locke grappled with the boundaries of reason and faith. They sought to reconcile scientific discoveries with religious beliefs, exploring how empirical evidence and spiritual insight could coexist. This period celebrated the human capacity for reason, yet it did not discard the importance of faith. Rather, it redefined it, suggesting that belief was not an absence of reason but a necessary complement to it. This era set the stage for a modern understanding where faith and reason are not adversaries but allies in the quest for truth.

In contemporary philosophy, figures like Alasdair MacIntyre have continued to explore this relationship, advocating for a synthesis that respects both rational inquiry and moral intuition. MacIntyre's virtue ethics emphasize the development of moral character through practical reason, suggesting that ethical living involves an integration of rational thought and virtuous action. This perspective reinforces the idea that reason and faith, when combined, offer a more comprehensive framework for understanding human existence. They provide not only a guide for moral behavior but also a means to engage with life's deeper questions.

Real-world examples further illustrate how faith and reason can operate in harmony. Consider the lives of scientists who maintain religious beliefs while pursuing empirical research. For them, the intricacies of the universe, revealed through scientific exploration, do not diminish their faith but enhance it. They see their work as a means of understanding the divine order, with each discovery a testament to the complexity and beauty of creation. Similarly, many religious institutions actively support scientific endeavors, recognizing the value of empirical knowledge in addressing global challenges and improving the human condition. These institutions often provide funding for research and education, fostering environments where science and spirituality coexist.

The integration of faith and reason offers numerous benefits, enriching both personal and collective understanding. Individuals who embrace this synthesis often experience a more profound sense of meaning, as they navigate life's complexities with both rational analysis and moral intuition. This integration enhances ethical decision-making, allowing individuals to draw on both logical reasoning and deeply held values when faced with moral dilemmas. It fosters personal growth, encouraging a holistic approach to life that values both the intellect and the spirit. By embracing both faith and reason, we open ourselves to a richer, more nuanced understanding of the world and our place within it.

Reflection Section

Consider your own experiences with faith and reason. Have there been moments when these forces have complemented each other in your life? Reflect on how integrating both perspectives might enhance your understanding and approach to the challenges you face. You might find it helpful to jot down your thoughts or discuss them with someone who shares your curiosity.

Cognitive Dissonance and Belief

Cognitive dissonance is a psychological concept you may experience when holding two conflicting beliefs, causing discomfort and tension. It's like trying to fit mismatched puzzle pieces together; something feels off, and it nags at you. In the realm of belief, especially when grappling with religious or spiritual ideas, cognitive dissonance can manifest when your deeply held convictions clash with new information or experiences. This inner conflict can be disorienting, prompting a reevaluation of what you thought you knew. Imagine questioning the nature of reality while holding onto a belief system that doesn't accommodate those questions—that's cognitive dissonance at play. This discomfort often compels individuals to seek resolution, as living in a state of dissonance is unsustainable long-term.

To navigate this tension, people employ various strategies to reconcile their beliefs with new insights. One common approach is selective exposure, where you might gravitate toward information that aligns with your existing beliefs, consciously or subconsciously filtering out contradictory viewpoints. This tendency can reinforce existing perspectives and provide temporary relief from dissonance. However, it may also prevent genuine growth and understanding. Another method involves critical reflection, where you actively engage with conflicting ideas, questioning and reevaluating your beliefs. This process can be challenging, requiring an openness to changing one's mind and embracing uncertainty. It's an exercise in intellectual humility, acknowledging that what you once held as truth may evolve in light of new evidence or perspectives. Both strategies highlight the dynamic nature of belief, underscoring the ongoing interplay between faith and reason.

Psychological studies offer insight into how cognitive dissonance influences belief systems. Experiments have shown that when individuals are faced with dissonance-inducing tasks, they often experience a shift in attitude to alleviate the discomfort. For instance, when participants are asked to advocate for a position they don't agree with, they may later adjust their beliefs to align more closely with their actions. This phenomenon suggests that dissonance can be a powerful catalyst for change, prompting a reassessment of previously held beliefs. It also highlights the complex relationship between action and belief, illustrating how external behaviors can influence internal convictions. These studies reveal that cognitive dissonance isn't merely a source of discomfort; it's also an opportunity for transformation.

Experiencing and resolving cognitive dissonance can lead to significant personal and spiritual growth. For some, the process of grappling with conflicting beliefs deepens their understanding of faith, prompting a more nuanced and mature perspective. Case studies of individuals who have navigated this terrain illustrate the potential for profound change. Consider someone raised in a strictly atheistic environment who begins to encounter spiritual experiences that challenge their worldview. As they wrestle with these contradictions, they may find themselves drawn to explore religious texts, engage in dialogue with believers, and ultimately arrive at a new understanding of faith that integrates both reason and experience. This journey is not without its challenges, but it offers the possibility of a richer, more comprehensive worldview.

Cognitive dissonance is not merely an obstacle to be overcome; it's a driving force for growth and discovery. By confronting and resolving the tension between conflicting beliefs, individuals can transition from a rigid adherence to dogma to a more open and flexible engagement with the world. This process encourages a lifelong commitment to learning, where beliefs are continuously refined and reevaluated in light of new experiences and insights. The capacity to embrace dissonance and use it as a tool for growth is a testament to the resilience and adaptability of the human spirit.

The Rationalist's Guide to Faith

Embracing a rationalist perspective on faith requires an approach that values critical inquiry and open-mindedness, providing a framework for understanding religious doctrines through logical analysis. At the core of this approach is the application of principles that guide you to assess claims with intellectual rigor. Begin with the basics: scrutinize religious texts and teachings with the same analytical tools used in other fields of study. Logical consistency, empirical evidence, and coherence with known facts become the benchmarks for evaluation. When faced with a religious claim, ask yourself: Does this align with established truths? Does it withstand reasoned scrutiny? Such questions help in discerning the validity of beliefs, allowing you to separate profound insights from unfounded assertions.

Rationalist thinkers have long engaged with faith, bringing nuanced perspectives to this complex relationship. Immanuel Kant, for instance, explored the limits and capabilities of human reason, particularly in his work on practical reason. Kant proposed that while empirical knowledge has its boundaries, moral and ethical considerations often point beyond what can be scientifically proven, suggesting a realm where faith may find its place. He argued that the existence of God, while not empirically provable, is a necessary postulate for the coherence of ethical life. This perspective invites you to consider that rationality does not exclude belief; instead, it provides a framework through which belief can be meaningfully interpreted and integrated into daily life.

Exploring faith through rational means requires tools that facilitate thoughtful reflection and analysis. Philosophical thought experiments, for example, can illuminate complex religious concepts by placing them in hypothetical scenarios. These exercises encourage you to question assumptions and explore the implications of beliefs in a structured manner. Another valuable tool is the scientific method, which, while primarily focused on empirical inquiry, can also guide the exploration of faith by promoting inquiry, hypothesis testing, and evidence evaluation. While faith may transcend empirical verification, applying a scientific mindset can lead to a deeper understanding of its impact on human experience and society.

However, engaging with faith from a rationalist standpoint presents challenges that require careful navigation. One such challenge is balancing skepticism with openness to spiritual experiences. It is natural to approach claims with a degree of doubt, especially when they lack immediate empirical evidence. Yet, maintaining an openness to experiences that fall outside the realm of logic allows for a fuller exploration of human existence. Consider the value of intuition and subjective experiences—often dismissed by strict rationalists—as they provide insights into aspects of life that elude quantification. Embracing a nuanced approach that respects both reason and the ineffable aspects of spirituality can lead to a more holistic understanding.

In the quest to reconcile faith and reason, you may encounter moments of tension, where the demands of logic seem to conflict with the pull of the spiritual. This is where the rationalist mindset truly shines, offering strategies for integrating these seemingly disparate aspects of life. By approaching faith with a spirit of inquiry rather than dogmatic adherence, you create space for growth and transformation. This journey involves continuously questioning and refining beliefs, recognizing that both faith and reason are dynamic forces that evolve over time. Rational engagement with faith is not about achieving certainty but embracing the complexity and richness of human belief.

Bridging the Divide: A Dialogue

In today's world, where the cacophony of competing ideas often drowns out meaningful discourse, fostering a dialogue between faith and reason becomes crucial. Imagine a space where scientists, theologians, philosophers, and laypeople sit side by side, united not by agreement but by a shared curiosity. Forums and conferences serve as these vital crossroads, inviting individuals from diverse backgrounds to engage in conversation. These gatherings are not about persuading others to adopt a singular viewpoint but about exploring the rich tapestry of human understanding. Through listening and sharing, participants gain insight into perspectives they may have never considered, fostering mutual respect and breaking down barriers that once seemed insurmountable.

Common ground emerges not from uniformity but from shared values and goals that transcend individual belief systems. Ethical concerns, such as environmental stewardship, provide a fertile ground for collaboration. Regardless of one's stance on the divine, the need to protect and nurture our planet resonates universally. This shared responsibility encourages partnerships between faith communities and scientific organizations, common in projects aimed at conserving natural resources and addressing climate change. These collaborations highlight how faith and reason can work together toward a common good, demonstrating that practical action often speaks louder than theoretical debates. The synergy of diverse perspectives enriches the dialogue, empowering participants to tackle complex challenges with creativity and compassion.

Examples of successful collaborations abound, showcasing how dialogue can lead to tangible outcomes. Consider interfaith initiatives that address global challenges like poverty, education, and healthcare. By pooling resources and expertise, these alliances achieve what might be impossible alone. In the scientific realm, interdisciplinary research projects often benefit from the input of theologians and ethicists, who provide valuable insights into the ethical implications of new technologies. These partnerships reflect a shared commitment to advancing human knowledge while respecting the moral and spiritual dimensions of innovation. They demonstrate that when faith and reason work hand in hand, they can pave the way for progress that honors both the mind and the heart.

Effective communication is the bedrock of any successful dialogue. It begins with active listening, where participants genuinely engage with others' ideas rather than merely waiting for their turn to speak. This requires an openness to being challenged and a willingness to adapt one's perspective. Empathetic engagement goes a step further, encouraging individuals to see the world through others' eyes. By acknowledging the emotions and experiences that shape beliefs, we create a space where empathy can flourish. Techniques such as reflective listening, where one restates what another has said to ensure understanding, can prevent miscommunication and build trust. These practices nurture an environment where dialogue thrives, fostering connections that transcend differences.

In promoting dialogue between faith and reason, we are reminded of the power of conversation to transform not only our understanding of the world but also our relationships with one another. It is through these exchanges that we find the courage to question, the humility to learn, and the wisdom to grow. As we engage with others, we discover that the divide between faith and reason is not as wide as it seems.

Embracing Uncertainty in Belief

In the complex tapestry of faith and reason, uncertainty often emerges as a key thread, weaving through and enriching our understanding of both domains. This uncertainty is not a flaw to be corrected but a space for exploration and growth. The concept of "faith seeking understanding" reflects this beautifully, suggesting an ongoing process where belief and inquiry coexist. It emphasizes that faith is not static; it evolves as we question and reflect. This dynamic interplay encourages humility, reminding us that our grasp of truth is always partial, always unfolding. Embracing uncertainty invites us to approach life's mysteries with open minds and willing hearts, ready to learn and adapt as new insights arise.

Philosophical and theological perspectives have long acknowledged the value of uncertainty in belief. Søren Kierkegaard, often regarded as the father of existentialism, championed the idea of the "leap of faith." He argued that true belief requires embracing the unknown, stepping into uncertainty without the safety net of empirical proof. Kierkegaard saw this leap not as irrational but as an authentic expression of faith, where certainty is not a prerequisite but a consequence of commitment. His views challenge the notion that belief must be grounded in complete certainty, suggesting instead that faith gains its strength from the courage to trust in the face of doubt. This perspective opens a space where both believers and skeptics can find common ground, acknowledging that uncertainty is inherent in the human condition.

Personal narratives often illustrate the transformative power of embracing uncertainty. Consider the testimony of a spiritual seeker who found strength precisely in the ambiguity of their beliefs. For them, the journey was not about arriving at definitive answers but about engaging with the questions themselves. This openness to uncertainty fostered a sense of curiosity and creativity, leading to unexpected insights and personal growth. Their story reveals that uncertainty can be a fertile ground for exploration, where the willingness to sit with ambiguity sparks new ways of thinking and being. It shows that by allowing ourselves to dwell in the unknown, we become more resilient, better equipped to handle life's unpredictability with grace and adaptability.

The benefits of accepting uncertainty extend beyond personal growth to include broader implications for how we engage with the world. Uncertainty fosters creativity, as the absence of fixed answers encourages us to think outside the box, to imagine possibilities we might otherwise overlook. It also cultivates curiosity, driving us to ask questions and seek knowledge, fueling a lifelong commitment to learning. This mindset transforms uncertainty from a source of anxiety into a wellspring of potential, where the unknown is not feared but embraced as a catalyst for discovery. Moreover, uncertainty builds resilience, teaching us to navigate change and challenge with flexibility, to adapt and thrive in an ever-evolving landscape.

As this chapter concludes, we recognize that embracing uncertainty is not a surrender to chaos but an invitation to engage deeply with life's complexities. It encourages us to live with an open heart and mind, ready to welcome new insights and experiences. This approach connects us to a larger journey of growth and understanding, where faith and reason walk hand in hand, each enhancing the other. In the next chapter, we will explore how ethics and morality intersect with belief, further examining the rich interplay of these foundational aspects of human existence.

Chapter Nine

The Future of Belief

Imagine a world where the touch of a screen opens doors to realms of spiritual exploration once limited to physical sanctuaries. In this digital age, the landscape of belief is undergoing a transformation, with technology playing a pivotal role in reshaping how we connect with spirituality. Whether you're a digital native or someone adapting to this rapid change, technology now offers new pathways to explore and engage with spiritual practices. The rise of online religious services and virtual worship communities exemplifies this shift. No longer confined by geography, individuals can now participate in religious rituals and services from the comfort of their homes. These digital gatherings provide access to a broad array of spiritual experiences, from live-streamed sermons to interactive prayer sessions, enabling communities to transcend physical boundaries. For many, this means not only maintaining ties to their faith but also discovering new avenues for spiritual growth.

Digital platforms have further enriched this experience by offering tools for meditation and mindfulness practices. Apps designed to enhance mental well-being, such as Headspace and Calm, have become popular resources for those seeking solace and introspection. These platforms provide guided meditations, breathing exercises, and daily reflections, allowing users to cultivate a sense of peace and mindfulness in their daily lives. The convenience of these apps makes it easier for individuals to incorporate spiritual practices into their routines, fostering a deeper connection to their inner selves. By offering meditation and mindfulness in an accessible format, they bridge the gap between traditional spiritual practices and modern lifestyles, inviting users to explore spirituality on their own terms.

Social media, too, plays a significant role in shaping contemporary belief systems. Platforms like Facebook, Instagram, and Twitter have become spaces for sharing spiritual insights and engaging in religious dialogues. Hashtags and viral campaigns focused on spirituality can spark conversations and connect like-minded individuals globally, creating vibrant online communities. Influencers and thought leaders often emerge within these digital spaces, shaping spiritual narratives and influencing followers' beliefs. They share personal experiences, insights, and teachings that resonate with their audiences, facilitating discussions that might not occur in traditional religious settings. However, the influence of social media on belief is not without its complexities. While it enables the spread of diverse ideas, it can also amplify extreme views and create echo chambers, where individuals are exposed only to beliefs that reinforce their existing perspectives. This dual nature of social media underscores the need for discernment and critical engagement when exploring spiritual content online.

Technological innovations have also transformed traditional spiritual practices and rituals, offering new ways to experience and understand religious concepts. Virtual reality (VR) experiences, for instance, provide immersive environments for religious education and exploration. Users can embark on virtual pilgrimages to sacred sites, participate in re-enactments of religious events, or engage in interactive lessons on theology and spirituality. Such experiences offer an unprecedented level of engagement, allowing individuals to explore their beliefs in a richly interactive and experiential manner. Meanwhile, artificial intelligence (AI) is being integrated into spiritual counseling and guidance, offering personalized insights and support to individuals seeking spiritual growth. AI-driven chatbots and virtual mentors provide users with tailored advice and resources, helping them navigate their spiritual journeys with greater clarity and confidence.

Despite the opportunities presented by technology, there are challenges to consider. One concern is the potential for digital disconnection, as virtual interactions might lack the depth and authenticity of face-to-face encounters. While online communities offer convenience and accessibility, they may not fully replicate the sense of belonging and connection found in physical gatherings. Ensuring that digital platforms complement rather than replace traditional spiritual communities is crucial for maintaining meaningful connections. Additionally, the sheer volume of spiritual content available online can be overwhelming, requiring individuals to develop discernment in selecting reliable sources amidst the noise.

Yet, the possibilities for increased access to diverse spiritual resources are vast. The internet provides a wealth of information, enabling individuals to explore a wide range of spiritual traditions and practices. From ancient philosophies to contemporary movements, the digital realm offers a treasure trove of knowledge for those seeking to expand their understanding of spirituality. This accessibility empowers individuals to tailor their spiritual journeys, drawing from diverse sources to create a personalized approach to belief. Whether exploring Eastern philosophies, indigenous practices, or modern spiritual movements, the digital world offers an inclusive space for exploration and growth.

Reflection Section: Exploring Spirituality in the Digital Age

As you navigate the digital landscape of spirituality, consider how technology has shaped your beliefs and practices. Reflect on the ways you engage with spiritual content online and the impact it has on your understanding of spirituality. Ask yourself:

- How have digital platforms influenced your spiritual exploration?

- What role do social media and influencers play in shaping your beliefs?

- How do you balance online engagement with traditional spiritual practices?

Journal your thoughts or discuss them with others to deepen your exploration of spirituality in the digital age.

Emerging Trends in Theistic Belief

In today's world, a fascinating array of new movements and belief systems are emerging, each with its distinct characteristics and goals. Among these, eco-spirituality and environmental theism are gaining significant traction. These movements view the natural world as sacred, emphasizing the interconnectedness of all living things and the divine presence within nature itself. They advocate for environmental stewardship as a form of spiritual practice, urging individuals to protect and preserve the Earth as a moral and religious duty. This perspective resonates with many who are increasingly concerned about climate change and environmental degradation, offering a spiritual dimension to ecological activism.

Alongside eco-spirituality, progressive religious movements are making waves by advocating for social justice and equality. These movements challenge traditional religious hierarchies and doctrines, emphasizing inclusivity and compassion. They often focus on issues such as racial and gender equality, LGBTQ+ rights, and economic justice, seeking to align their spiritual beliefs with contemporary social values. This approach appeals to those who feel alienated from conventional religious institutions, offering a more relevant and socially engaged form of spirituality. By integrating activism with faith, these movements provide a powerful platform for individuals to express their beliefs through action, fostering a sense of purpose and community.

Demographic shifts are also playing a crucial role in shaping the landscape of theistic belief. As younger generations come of age, they bring with them new attitudes and perspectives that challenge traditional religious norms. Millennials and Generation Z, in particular, tend to prioritize authenticity and inclusivity, seeking spiritual experiences that reflect their diverse identities and values. This generational shift has led to an increasing diversity of religious expressions in urban areas, where multiculturalism and pluralism are more prevalent. Cities become melting pots of belief, where individuals from different backgrounds exchange ideas and practices, creating vibrant spiritual communities that transcend cultural and religious boundaries.

The impact of interfaith marriages on belief systems is another notable trend. As people from different religious backgrounds form families, they often blend their traditions, creating unique hybrid spiritual practices. These marriages can lead to a greater appreciation for diverse beliefs, fostering tolerance and understanding. Children raised in interfaith households are exposed to multiple perspectives from an early age, which can encourage open-mindedness and a broader worldview. This blending of traditions reflects the evolving nature of belief in a globalized world, where rigid boundaries between religions become increasingly porous.

Interdisciplinary approaches are further influencing new theistic beliefs by integrating insights from various fields. Neuroscience, for example, has shed light on the physiological aspects of mystical experiences, revealing how certain brain states correlate with feelings of transcendence and connection. This scientific perspective offers a deeper understanding of spiritual experiences, validating them as genuine phenomena rooted in the brain's complex workings. Anthropology, too, contributes to our understanding of indigenous spiritual practices, highlighting the rich diversity of belief systems across cultures. By studying these practices, scholars gain insights into the universal human quest for meaning, revealing common threads that unite disparate traditions.

Globalization continues to shape the evolution of theistic beliefs, as the blending of Eastern and Western spiritual traditions creates new, syncretic forms of spirituality. Eastern practices such as meditation, yoga, and mindfulness have gained popularity in the West, influencing how individuals approach spirituality and self-care. This cross-cultural exchange enriches spiritual practices, offering a more holistic and integrated approach to well-being. Additionally, global religious movements are adapting to local cultural contexts, incorporating indigenous beliefs and customs to resonate with diverse populations. This adaptability ensures that spiritual practices remain relevant and accessible, inviting individuals to engage with belief systems that honor their cultural heritage while embracing universal truths. As these trends continue to evolve, they reflect the dynamic and ever-changing nature of belief in the contemporary world.

The Journey Continues: Faith in a Changing World

Consider the fluid nature of personal belief as a reflection of your life's unfolding narrative. Just as a river carves its path through varied landscapes, your spiritual beliefs evolve, shaped by experiences and transitions. Throughout life, personal narratives of faith are not static; they grow, shift, and adapt. Imagine a person who, in their youth, embraced atheism with conviction, only to find themselves, decades later, opening to the possibility of a divine presence. This evolution might unfold through subtle shifts, like the influence of a meaningful relationship or the profound impact of a life-altering event. Such transitions serve as pivotal moments, prompting introspection and reevaluation of long-held beliefs.

Life transitions, whether joyous or challenging, often act as catalysts for spiritual reflection and growth. Consider the birth of a child, which might inspire a deeper exploration of spirituality, as new parents ponder the mysteries of life and creation. Conversely, the loss of a loved one can lead to a quest for understanding, driving individuals to seek solace and meaning in spiritual practices. These transitions compel us to confront existential questions, encouraging a reassessment of our beliefs and values. Through this process, we cultivate resilience, developing a more nuanced understanding of our place in the world.

In our rapidly changing society, traditional beliefs face numerous challenges, prompting reevaluation and adaptation. Scientific advancements continually reshape our understanding of the universe, challenging literal interpretations of religious texts. As we unravel the mysteries of the cosmos and delve into the intricacies of human consciousness, questions arise about the relevance of ancient doctrines in explaining contemporary phenomena. These challenges spark dialogue, inviting believers to explore the intersection of faith and science, seeking ways to reconcile traditional teachings with modern discoveries.

This dialogue often reveals tensions between traditional doctrines and modern ethical perspectives. Issues such as gender equality, LGBTQ+ rights, and social justice challenge long-standing religious norms, prompting faith communities to reflect on their values and practices. In response, some communities embrace inclusivity and diversity, striving to create spaces that welcome all individuals, regardless of their identity or background. These initiatives demonstrate the resilience of faith communities, highlighting their ability to adapt and thrive amidst societal changes. By fostering open-minded exploration and dialogue, these communities pave the way for a more inclusive and compassionate spiritual landscape.

Faith communities that have successfully navigated these challenges often serve as beacons of hope and inspiration. They demonstrate that traditional beliefs can coexist with modern values, evolving to meet the needs of contemporary society. Consider a religious congregation that, in response to environmental concerns, integrates ecological stewardship into its spiritual practices. By aligning their beliefs with global challenges, they reaffirm their commitment to the well-being of the planet, fostering a sense of collective responsibility and purpose. Similarly, community-based responses to social and environmental challenges underscore the potential for faith to drive positive change, uniting individuals in pursuit of a common good.

In this spirit, I encourage you to embark on a journey of open-minded exploration, embracing uncertainty and growth. Lifelong learning is vital to spiritual development, inviting you to continuously question, reflect, and expand your understanding of the world. By engaging with diverse spiritual paths and perspectives, you cultivate empathy and broaden your horizons, gaining insights that enrich your own beliefs. Interfaith dialogue, in particular, offers a valuable opportunity to connect with others, fostering mutual respect and understanding across cultural and religious divides.

As you navigate this landscape of spiritual exploration, remember that the journey is not about reaching a definitive destination. Rather, it is about embracing the process of growth and transformation, allowing your beliefs to evolve in response to new experiences and insights. This ongoing journey invites you to remain open to the mysteries of existence, nurturing a sense of wonder and curiosity that transcends the boundaries of tradition and modernity. By cultivating an open heart and mind, you embark on a path of discovery that leads to a deeper understanding of yourself and the world around you.

Conclusion

As we come to the end of this intellectual and spiritual journey, I invite you to pause and reflect on the path we've traveled together. Throughout these pages, we've explored the complex tapestry of belief, unraveling the threads of reason, faith, and personal experience that shape our understanding of the world. We've delved into the stories of individuals who, like you, have grappled with life's profound questions, finding solace and meaning in their unique journeys from atheism to belief in God.

At the heart of this exploration lies a fundamental truth: the quest for understanding is a deeply human endeavor, one that transcends the boundaries of culture, tradition, and ideology. Whether you find yourself firmly rooted in faith or still navigating the uncharted waters of doubt, the insights and experiences shared in this book offer a compass to guide your journey. The philosophical arguments, scientific discoveries, and personal testimonies we've encountered serve as signposts, illuminating the diverse paths that lead to a deeper appreciation of the divine.

As you reflect on these pages, I encourage you to embrace the power of curiosity and open-mindedness. Just as the individuals whose stories grace these chapters have demonstrated, growth often lies in the willingness to question, to explore, and to engage with perspectives that challenge our preconceptions. By cultivating a spirit of intellectual humility and empathy, you open yourself to the possibility of transformation, allowing your beliefs to evolve in response to new insights and experiences.

Beyond personal growth, the lessons of this book extend to the realm of human connection. In a world that often feels divided by differences, the art of respectful dialogue and understanding becomes a beacon of hope. By engaging with others whose beliefs and experiences differ from your own, you contribute to the creation of a more compassionate and inclusive society. Whether through interfaith initiatives, community service, or simple acts of kindness, you have the power to build bridges of understanding, fostering a world where diversity is celebrated as a source of strength and wisdom.

As an author, my deepest hope is that this book has served as a catalyst for your own journey of discovery. The questions and ideas explored within these pages are not meant to provide definitive answers but rather to ignite a spark of curiosity that propels you forward. I encourage you to continue seeking, questioning, and engaging with the mysteries of existence, knowing that the path to understanding is a lifelong adventure. Embrace the challenges and joys of this journey, and trust in the resilience of your own spirit to guide you.

In the end, the story of belief is one that unfolds within the heart of each individual. It is a tale of courage, compassion, and the unending search for meaning in a complex world. As you embark on the next chapter of your own journey, I invite you to carry with you the insights and inspiration found within these pages. Let them serve as a reminder of the extraordinary potential that lies within each of us—the potential to learn, to grow, and to make a positive impact on the world around us.

So I ask you, dear reader, what will be the next step in your journey of understanding? How will you harness the power of reason, faith, and human connection to create a life of purpose and meaning? The answers to these questions lie within you, waiting to be discovered. As you continue on your path, know that you are part of a global community of seekers, united by a shared desire to unravel the mysteries of existence and to build a world of greater compassion and understanding.

REASON TO BELIEVE

With an open heart and a curious mind, I invite you to embrace the adventure that awaits. The future of belief is yours to shape, and the possibilities are limitless. May your journey be filled with wonder, wisdom, and the joy of discovery. Thank you for joining me on this extraordinary exploration of the human spirit.

About the Author

Sawsan Charif is a passionate educator, speaker, and author whose work bridges the gap between intellect and intuition, reason and wonder. As the founder of **Brain Corner Publishing**, she creates books and courses that empower readers to grow in confidence, communication, and clarity—whether they are learning English, refining their public speaking skills, or exploring the mysteries of belief and consciousness.

Fluent in multiple languages and drawing from a background in law, education, and leadership, Sawsan teaches Business English, public speaking, and personal development to students and professionals around the world. Her dynamic approach combines academic insight with practical tools, all rooted in deep empathy for the modern learner and seeker.

Sawsan is the author of over a dozen books, including *Public Speaking Mastery, English Swear Words & Slang for ESL Learners, Fluent with ChatGPT, Business Communication, Dialectical Behavior Therapy,* and *Reason to Believe.* Her upcoming titles explore cutting-edge topics like peptides, cryptocurrency, and ancient mysteries — always with the goal of making complex topics accessible, actionable, and transformative.

When she's not writing, teaching, or guiding others through transformative learning, you'll find her researching ancient texts, designing curriculum for her online academy, or sipping tea in quiet reflection—always seeking the next thread of truth to weave into her work.

To explore more of her books, programs, and upcoming releases, visit Or join the email list for exclusive content and early access to new books. sawsan@brain cornerpublishing.com

References

Adams, R. (1987). *The virtue of faith*. Oxford University Press.

Anselm. (n.d.). Ontological argument for God's existence. *Internet Encyclopedia of Philosophy*.

Aquinas, T. (n.d.). Five ways to prove the existence of God. *California State University, Long Beach*.

Boston University Medical Campus. (n.d.). *The neuroscience of religious experience*.

Britannica. (n.d.). *New religious movement (NRM): Definition, types, & facts*.

Church Notes App. (n.d.). *How does technology influence religion and spirituality?*

Decety, J., et al. (2019). Religious upbringing associated with less altruism, study finds. *University of Chicago*.

Downing, D. C. (2002). *The most reluctant convert: C.S. Lewis's journey to faith*. InterVarsity Press.

Evans, C. S. (2014). Moral arguments for the existence of God. *Stanford Encyclopedia of Philosophy*.

Evans, C. S. (2015). The evolution of theisms: The four technological revolutions and the four theistic revolutions. *Scientific Research Publishing*.

Fair Latter Day Saints. (2005). "Believest thou...?": Faith, cognitive dissonance, and the psychology of religious experience.

Hervieux-Moore, G. (2021). Religious literacy: Civic education for a common good. *Religion & Education, 48*(1), 22–34.

Hipps, S. (2006). The impact of social media on belief formation. *IDEAS/RePEc*.

Integral Church. (2012). *15 great principles shared by all religions*.

Integrative Psychology. (n.d.). *Secularity's influence on the moral compass of society*.

John15.Rocks. (n.d.). *11 intellectuals atheists who became Christians.*

Kierkegaard, S. (n.d.). *Stanford Encyclopedia of Philosophy.*

Lima, E., & Holt, J. (2006). The God delusion by Richard Dawkins - Books - Review. *The New York Times.*

MacIntyre, A. (n.d.). Virtue ethics. *Saylor Academy.*

Miessler, D. (n.d.). *The principles of secular humanism.*

National Catholic Register. (n.d.). *St. Thomas Aquinas: Harmony between faith and reason.*

Oxford Academic. (n.d.). *Psychology of religious conversion and spiritual transformation.*

Pew Research Center. (2008). *What brain science tells us about religious belief.*

Pew Research Center. (2020). *On the intersection of science and religion.*

Plantinga, A. (n.d.). *Faith and rationality: Reason and belief in God.* Princeton University.

Pluralism Project. (n.d.). *Interfaith dialogue.* Harvard University.

PMC. (n.d.). *Religious communities and human flourishing.*

PMC. (n.d.). *Spirituality but not religiosity is associated with better health.*

Polkinghorne, J. (n.d.). *Quantum physics and theology.* Yale University Press.

Science Direct. (2020). How cultural learning and cognitive biases shape religious beliefs. *Current Opinion in Psychology, 40,* 73–77.

Stanford Encyclopedia of Philosophy. (n.d.). Atheism and agnosticism.

Stanford Encyclopedia of Philosophy. (n.d.). Religious experience.

Taylor & Francis Online. (2021). A critical review of Maslow's theory of spirituality. *The International Journal of Transpersonal Studies, 40*(1).

Verywellmind. (n.d.). *Existential crisis: What it is and how to cope.*

Wikipedia. (n.d.). *Religious interpretations of the Big Bang theory.*

Wikipedia. (n.d.). *Relationship between religion and science.*

Wikipedia. (n.d.). *Secular morality.*

Wikipedia. (n.d.). *Watchmaker analogy.*